Sam Helio

Surviving Domestic Abuse

Michael Terence Publishing

This edition first published in paperback by
Michael Terence Publishing in 2022
www.mtp.agency

Copyright © 2022 Sam Helio

Sam Helio has asserted the right to be identified as
the author of this work in accordance with the
Copyright, Designs and Patents Act 1988

ISBN 9781800943889

No part of this publication may be reproduced, stored
in a retrieval system, or transmitted, in any form or
by any means, electronic, mechanical, photocopying,
recording or otherwise, without the prior
permission of the publisher

Cover images
Copyright © Artur Nichiporenko
www.123rf.com

Cover design
Copyright © 2022 Michael Terence Publishing

*For the African Caribbean Care Group, Hulme, Manchester
where shared experiences gave me perspective*

Contents

EPISODE 1
Trouble In Paradise 1

EPISODE 2 Cries:
A Beautiful Voice Is Not Enough 27

EPISODE 3
Welcome To Hell In Desire 63

EPISODE 4
Crises 131

EPISODE 5
For Whom The Bell Tolls 187

EPISODE 6
Specific Overtures? 225

EPISODE 7
Everlasting Ache 291

Acknowledgements 323

About the Author 325

EPISODE 1

Trouble In Paradise

His name is Red, and that describes his temper. My name is Blue, and that describes my mood. Red Hawk and Blue Sirocco.

When the police told me Red would end up killing me, I had to act. It was now or never if I was going to survive. But how?

We lived in a city named Desire. Still do. That's not the name you know it by. I could have named it *Home Town* or *Our Town* but those names have already been taken. I named it Desire to protect innocents like me who've suffered domestic abuse. Also, to conceal the names of police officers, judges, court officials and social workers whom I criticise, just in case I need their services in future.

You might say I'm hedging my bets.

As for my name for a city, well it conjures up what many folks desire - gold, ladies of the night and the souls of men. And again, like a song tells us in the 1950's musical, *The Boy Friend*, "a love affair is delightful anywhere."

And there's another, more bitter reason, for the name: domestic abuse happens up and down the land, not just in one specific place. So, if you've experienced domestic abuse at first hand, any city named Desire is surely your home town, too.

To tell you my story, and maybe yours, I've borrowed techniques from straight theatre, such as a narrator coming to the front of the stage with a soliloquy, revealing his thoughts, that's me; abrupt dramatisations of personal crises and domestic violence as in horror stories, and official statistics. I do this to break down the distinction between what happens in the novel and the wider truth about domestic abuse across our nation. Yes, the novel is make-believe based on acute personal experience but its wider implications are about a modern social scourge.

I'm not pretending this is a self-help book, inviting you to trawl through a digest of psychological consensus of how abused people can escape their tormentors. It's my record of what I endured, my mistakes as well as my solution to my outsize domestic problem.

Dare you read more and experience hell on earth in a city named Desire?

Red, my abuser, was an angry boy all right. You could tell this the moment you saw him. He used to have his hair cut in angry style like King Henry V, a pudding bowl of hair from ear to ear, continuing the upturned bowl shape with lower back and sides shaved away. He combed his hair forward at the front in a Beatles' style mop.

Then there was his angry way of looking at you. His eyes might stare harshly to confront strangers in pubs with his threatening presence, a trick that worked nicely in the regions [I do not say provinces] but never in London where no one gave a fig, no matter how timid or frail they were. Red would survey a face surreptitiously as if to gauge the emotional weather brewing under the skin. If his target noticed him, Red would quickly glance away. However threatening he looked to most people in Desire, Red's face would become fearful and go all of a quiver when faced with probing by benefits officers.

When we first met in the Glass House, a mixed bar that was near my flat and which became our local, strands of need and hope drew us together. We had both suffered a recent bereavement. I was also recovering from a failed relationship, more flicker than flame. Red had been a baker in his teens and, when he broke up with a girl, he'd turned to painting and decorating. I was a generation older than him, a retired teacher living modestly on my pension.

I know people wondered what on earth we both had in common. Well, Red and I were both fatherless. Yes, our fathers had sex to sow us into our mothers. But

Red's father didn't stick around for his birth. Mine abandoned me when I was six.

Red didn't mind my age nor my being disabled. I was already designated blind because of a regressive eye condition, which sporadic surgery had stalled but not cured. Sometimes I could see, sometimes I couldn't, just a mix of blacks and browns if it was dark or lemons and creams if it was light. When I could see, what I saw was distorted and incomplete.

When Red and I first got together, we couldn't know that Red would become disabled later through his own recklessness.

That comes later in this story.

What could I give Red that he couldn't get elsewhere? Well, all I had to offer was my scholarly talk and amateur lovemaking. In the beginning, we held one another like footballers rocking after scoring a goal. It wasn't everlastingly romantic. Our bodies touched like squelchy blobs. He took my face in his hands, caressing my hairy cheeks with his stubby fingers.

"Talk to me, darling. Make me feel better."

For a time, I was grateful for the warmth and sweetness of his words. When I felt his tongue with mine, his tongue was raw from his endless whiskies of the night.

Well, that may be. Although love may join us humans at first, it divides us later on. Love-making may seem ecstatic, even luxurious, to begin with, but you can't keep this luxury forever. Our fanciful elevation of sex as heaven on earth might have slithered into a different, more durable affection; mighty Aphrodite with the sex left out. That's the conventional wisdom. However, if one of you is determined on sex forever, the desire may turn into inexhaustible lust and then spiral into hell on earth. That is if your mutual love and companionship aren't destroyed by housekeeping, housework and child-rearing.

After a year together, I asked Red, "Will you love me when I'm old and fat?"

"I do," was his reply.

Before we started Red could have had more than his fair share of bargain-basement one-night stands. But that was not what he wanted. He had had an older lover, whom he met in a public toilet when he was barely twenty. They had been together for twelve years, a period Red always looked back on as an idyll and far superior to anything later. It can't have been that lovely because the alcoholic partner died of cirrhosis of the liver. Red hankered after another twelve years' repeat of the fondly misremembered idyll with plenty of sex on tap, money spent like flowing water and psychological control of the replacement partner.

As to unmistakable signs of trouble in paradise, well, anyone who's had a love affair learns that when two people are together, they don't love one another equally. Red started asking me whom I had sex with before him. Then how much I had loved them, more or less than I loved him? And so on. No matter how clear my answers, he was never satisfied.

ADVICE

Partners who've been together for some time will find it difficult, no, impossible to find anything new to whisper in one another's ears. So, it comes down to: "Do you still love me?" "Are you still happy?"

Is that the best any of us can do?

***

So it was with Red and me as time wore on. After three years rarely did we lie in one another's arms. Yet Red insisted on kisses to replace sweet nothings. He couldn't distinguish between his emotional needs and passion.

When he was away from me and drinking away the day with his buddies, as one of them told me later, he showed them how obsessed he was with me.

"He never stops talking about you. It's Blue this and Blue that all through the fucking afternoon. Drives everyone nuts."

Red had psychological needs, sure enough, needs like companionship, encouragement and, when he was with me, a sense of belonging. I learnt that some of Red's problems stemmed from his family. He had grown up in an atmosphere without tenderness. When I tried to be affectionate, he resisted me. You see, lack of tenderness in the way Red was brought up had deprived his soul of the air of life.

But, whatever my own inner conflicts and unresolved emotions, when the passion between Red and me was spent, I wasn't violent, ever. Red was.

At first, he transferred his need for emotional expression into another obsession, not football in general but Manchester United on and off the pitch. As a loyal Red, when he watched a Manchester United game either (on rare occasions) on BBC1, or when it was on Sky at a nearby pub, he did so with intense concentration, weighing up the pros and cons of the talent and the contest, especially early in the Premiership season when there were thirty-plus games ahead. Later in the season, it was a tunnel-vision obsession.

Red's illusion of fulfilment through Manchester

United possessed him. It swelled his sense of himself and misled him to other follies. But his sublimation - that's the correct psychological term - through his commitment as an ultra-loyal fan of Man U could not, however, compensate for Red's frustrated sexual desires. And the combination of that frustration, his lack of tenderness, and his increasing alcoholism was strangling what was left of his compassion. If you saw him sitting in a pub, silent, in repose, you could see that his natural expression was bleak and impassive.

When he got angry, Red turned first to using harsh words to inflict emotional wounds on me. To poke fun at us because we were two men kissing, he taunted my first name, changing it into "Blue Belle, Blue Belle." Then came violence. I had osteoarthritis in my wrist and hands. He would twist them to ratchet up the pain.

No longer could I greet my lover with delight. Instead, my mind was rocked with dawning apprehension turning into abject fear as to what was next in store for me. So, our brief days of delight dwindled into years of despair. I felt I was caught in the eye of some psychological storm that I didn't understand. I felt increasing, acute fright. But I knew I had to take a grip on myself to deal with the damage and survive.

Late one Friday night after hours of heavy drinking, Red burst into our flat positively quivering with unexplained, inexplicable rage. He smiled, a frightening grimace as if worse horror was lurking within him waiting to be unleashed.

He began, "Don't tell me how I'm feeling, how I'm behaving. I work my ass off to get this horrible flat ready for - for what? And when I'm almost done you say it isn't good enough."

I had never said any such thing but all I did was ask a question,

"Red, what's wrong? What's eating you?"

My words were useless. There was no point in my trying to be reasonable or to placate him. All I saw was flint in his eyes as I looked at his grim-set face. But I tried again.

"Red, just calm down."

"You shut your gob. You're tempting flies. You used to teach at some high school and you're a mine of misinformation. Well, thanks a heap. I can always use a nice, unprejudiced opinion. Let me get this clear. You've spoken and that's the end of the matter. Everyone else can just shut their gobs. You've made up your mind. You don't want to know the facts."

"I don't know what the facts are. I don't know what's

got into you."

He couldn't contain his sudden fury except by banging on the bedroom door. Then he opened it and banged it shut.

I still don't know the trigger that had set him off that night. But I should have taken it as a warning, the shape of things to come.

5 CATEGORIES OF DOMESTIC ABUSE

Stepping back now, I can see this as beginning a general pattern of domestic abuse.

An official list of fault lines by the commissioner for domestic violence on her website covers behaviour all too familiar to us victims. The ones that I endured were:

1 Red insulting and humiliating me in public;
2 making me think I was crazy or stupid;
3 trivial attempts at emotional blackmail in the sense of exposing in public things that were embarrassing; you can fill in your own idiosyncrasies.

And others would follow such as

4 isolating me from friends. I have no living family.

The running undercurrent was

5 creating a sense of impending punishment.

***

But in the beginning, I didn't understand these things. And I wasn't any wiser two nights later, which was a Sunday.

I don't know how that began either, the scrap between Red and the doorman on the street outside what was now our favourite pub, the Glass House. But I felt the consequences, sure enough.

I'd spent an uneventful, even cordial, evening there with Red. Then I slipped out of the bar to get some fresh air. When I turned around, Red and the doorman were at one another's throats, full throttle as it were. This doorman had huge arms like slabs of meat in an old-fashioned butcher's shop and a massive gut to match. The two of them clattered out of the pub vestibule and out along the pavement to the cobbled area in front of the local canal.

"Stop! Stop! You're killing one another!" I called. I felt silly. I was inadequate.

The doorman gave Red a brutish, open-handed push to his chest. Red stumbled two steps backwards and then fell sprawling over a stray metal chair. He thudded to the cobbles, scraping his arms.

People were passing this way and that along the pavement but no one would stop. Red and the doorman were still pushing and pulling one another by their hair, their arms and shoulders, until the doorman wrested himself free and shoved Red onto the ground, banging his head on the hard cobbles.

A tall snooty passer-by stopped to give his verdict,

"People who cruise around the canal end up floating in it. We all float there sooner or later. That includes the two of you, bruvs."

"Give me a break," said the tousled doorman as he stood up to his full height and shook his clothes free from Red whom he saw as an inconvenient troll.

Red, now sitting up, certainly looked the worse for wear. He was pouring with sweat, his Henry V hair-do was glued to his temples and forehead. The ultra-camp duty manager of the pub came out to see what was what. He wouldn't let Red back in and said with mincing severity,

"You always take on new doormen; try and make their life hell. Move on. The two of you [meaning me as well] are blocking the pavement."

An unknown woman with the jaw of a prize fighter who was finishing a fag, said consolingly,

"Don't take it to heart. The staff probably got a good hard-on while they were watching the fight. Just kidding," she added as if to soften the manager's glare.

As she leant back on one of the scrubby trees

dotting the pavement, one of the lower branches stirred by the sharp breeze whipped and smacked her. Then she tottered back into the pub.

Her half cigarette lay on the edge of the pavement, its smoking front twinkling capriciously. Red picked it up, gave it another pull then, disgusted with himself, spat it out. A man with a weak chin and a trendy cloth cap came along and stamped on it. Then he also picked it up. He was about to hand it to Red, saying angrily, "Take it, litter lout, and dispose of it responsibly!"

But the man changed his mind. Instead, he took Red's hand and stubbed the spent fag into his palm.

"Don't do it again," the rude man said contemptuously. "Say it: 'I won't do it again.'"

"Like hell, I will," Red replied. "And get the fuck off me. Keep your hands to yourself, paedo."

I led Red home. He wouldn't go quietly. He turned on me.

"Do you think I'm gonna beat you to death, you fucking scared rabbit? Should I call you Tits 'cos of where you wobble above, or Guts for where you wobble below?

"You're an old-timer. Remember that old TV commercial about waistlines? Sure, you do: 'If you can pinch more than an inch,' or how many more inches for you, three, seven, ten?"

"Better stop now, Red."

"Or what, Old Tits?"

A convertible car with the hood down trundled past on the opposite side of the road. The driver was old, his wife was older. They stopped and turned their heads to look at the pitiful scene, us, the plebs. Then they turned back to face the road ahead and moved on.

"What the fuck you looking at, you old queers?" Red yelled at the car as he gave them a V sign. "Did you get a boner? Was it big enough?"

When I grimaced at his gesture, Red resumed his verbal attack on me.

"What'ya gonna do? Think I'm scared of you? Call the police. See if I care. It took three of them to hold me down in the pub last time. Want an encore? I'm waiting. Want to test it now? You're supposed to be good at exams, in and out of school."

Just for relief, I looked up at the cloudless black sky, powdered with bright stars. Then I lost my balance on the sloping pavement. My feet slipped and down I went, rolling and sliding, hurting my hand against the stone front of the closed HSBC bank on the corner. My poor eyesight went completely. Everything looked as dark as a well.

"Oh! I've killed you, the fearless leader of the shit hole you call home," said Red triumphantly.

I tried to get up. I fell back again. I raised myself a little, steadying myself with my hands and knees. I knew what I must have looked like, a startled deer caught in the headlights of a lorry.

Red was not sympathetic.

"Don't you dare give me any of your shit. I ain't taking more shit from anyone else tonight."

I hoisted myself up and, as my wobbly eyesight came back, we moved on down dark streets. I glanced at the side streets and little alleys. The doorways to shops and offices, hooded like gothic crevices, reminded me of the shattered dreams of our damaged lives, Red's and mine. I reflected on how we humans are children of the landscape around us. And how it imprisons us in the unforgiving lessons it has taught us.

Red was still fuming about his fight with the doorman. He wanted more action and right now.

As soon as we got back to our building and into the flat it was a case of, "Ouch!"

For Red had just punched my face. Then he shoved me into the wall between the main room and the kitchen. He stood with an aggressive slouch, holding a can of lager from the fridge in one hand. What was the point of trying to tell him things he couldn't think through for himself?

I didn't know where he cut me but blood started to trickle from somewhere in my hair. When I stumbled, Red kicked my right leg. I lost my balance for the second time that night and fell. I flopped on the floor like a discarded teddy bear. What made it worse was how I felt, tossed aside like rubbish in the gutter.

Red's next targets were my beloved pictures, outsize posters from exhibitions and tourist centres that I had loved: the Kremlin with its gilt dome cathedrals from an exhibition of Russian art at the Guggenheim Museum in New York; a montage of architectural drawings of famous buildings, one across Italy and the other in Venice, posters bought in the Termini Station in Rome.

Red didn't want to destroy the Venice poster, only the glass in the outsize frame. He thumped his clenched fist into the glass again and again. He didn't just break the glass but splintered his skin until he cut his clenched fist. His blood oozed from myriad tiny scratches. Shards of glass cascaded onto the laminate floor.

"Why on earth did you do that?" I asked, trembling as I spoke.

"Because I fucking felt like it, blockhead."

I tried to hold my nerve. But think how awkward it is

to get glass shards and splinters into a neat pile to be brushed into a dustpan before they disperse themselves around a room. That's bad enough. But, as I tried to do just that, Red took swipes at my head from above while adding cutting comments: "You old blind cunt" [swipe]; "You old blind arsehole" [swipe]; "Don't you know how heaving with shit your old arsehole is? [swipe]." He raised his fists and shook them at me, "You're a cocksucker. And not a very good one."

I couldn't wait for calm to get the glass fragments together. If they scattered, then the floor would become a minefield. And I had to shield my head from Red's blows and my fingers from the splinters.

To add comedy and incongruity to my perilous situation, my false teeth tumbled out of my mouth and clattered on the laminate floor. I'm telling you straight, dentures don't obey you, even when they're in your own mouth.

Red's momentary reign of terror couldn't last much longer, could it? He must tire. I must get the glass fragments together. It mustn't take all night.

Once you've had the abrupt shock of a first punch or slap, you might take stock of this crucial shift in your domestic circumstances. Psychological violence has crossed a border into physical assault. You might be thinking, 'I never thought he'd use violence against me.' So, let's try and clarify things.

2 MAJOR PRINCIPLES WE NEED TO MAKE CLEAR ABOUT DOMESTIC VIOLENCE

1 If violence against women is unacceptable and inexcusable, and almost all of us think that is so, shouldn't violence against men also be unacceptable and inexcusable?
2 Domestic violence has damaging consequences. Whether the victim is a woman or a man, their belief in their worth will get eroded by continuous abuse.

5 WRONG HEADED EXCUSES FOR DOMESTIC VIOLENCE

There are many common beliefs about why people choose to be violent. Here are some regular ones:

1. They came from a broken home; [or this variant on the same theme]: They had a disturbed, traumatic childhood;
2. It's drink or drugs that make them violent;
3. They can't express their feelings in words. That's why they take their frustrations out on their partners;
4. They have problems with managing anger. They simply can't control their anger;

5 [And perhaps most insulting of all]: There's something so irritating about you that it gets under their skin and drives them insane, turns them to violence.

Remember, these are excuses.

ADVICE
3 REASONS TO TURN FACT INTO FICTION

1 This story set in Desire might resonate with you, especially if the abuse you've had to put up with came to a climax during lockdown for Covid-19. This story takes place in 2020, the year of Covid and Covid restrictions, and 2021, the year of haphazard relief when spring came.

I can hear you ask, and it's my question, too, 'Why did I ever start a novel about domestic abuse?'

It's not a barrel of laughs, far from it. But I felt the need to share my own poignant experience of abuse while the memories and pain were still sharp, to set down a record. The core of this novel is an unusual phenomenon: domestic abuse where both abuser and abused are disabled. My intention is to dramatize a threatening situation, the abuse I survived, and draw productive conclusions from it.

2 But if everything is based on cold, hard facts,

obstinate things, as US President Ronald Regan once remarked, then why did I turn fact into fiction by writing a novel instead of a memoir?

My reasons, besides recording my physical and psychological abuse, are: I target a few of our cherished social institutions for their failure over the years to help resolve the abuse against me (and by implication any of you who have also suffered). While I was trapped and afraid, I could not have set down a clear record with incidents and dates about repeated ridicule and denials of help with the pinpoint accuracy of a diarist. Put another way, what I have to say might not stand up in court if our hallowed institutions took up the cudgels of the law against me. But facts into fiction in this novel might cut through indifference when facts alone don't.

However, rather than call the sections in the book *chapters* as I might with a regular novel, I call them *episodes* since they each describe Red's downward cycle in terms of the episodes of his violence and my ascending attempt to break free. In each episode, I offer advice to you based on what the experience taught me.

3 Perhaps you're skimming these opening pages and trying to decide whether the book is worth your

while reading it. You may be wondering if you can trust me to show you something interesting and useful about combatting domestic abuse.

For that to happen, my story about surviving domestic abuse has to be relevant to you. I hope you haven't endured domestic abuse yourself, but it's likely you know someone who has, someone in your family perhaps, or someone you know at work or whom you've heard about.

5 CORE PRINCIPLES TO GET TO GRIPS WITH

Let's start with the basics. I've looked up definitions on the web. They repeat and elaborate what I wrote earlier:

1 Domestic abuse goes beyond physical violence, being hit or beaten. It includes repeated forms of abusive behaviour to maintain power and control in a relationship. Such abuse may be carried out by a partner, an ex-partner or a member of your family. The government's definition of domestic violence and abuse recognises this. To sum up, it defines domestic abuse as:

"Any incident or pattern of incidents of controlling, coercive, threatening behaviour, violence or abuse between those aged 16 or over who are, or have been, intimate partners or family members regardless of gender or sexuality. It can encompass, but is not limited to, the following types of abuse: psychological, physical, sexual, financial and emotional."

I hope this definition reaches you. If you've experienced domestic abuse, you've had a bitter education.

2 Going beyond physical abuse (which is easier to understand), the goal of psychological abuse is coercive control. That means a pattern of intimidation, degradation, isolation and control within physical or sexual violence. So, there is psychological and emotional abuse as well as physical violence. And any of these can lead to financial or economic abuse.

How does this fit in with the general scheme of domestic abuse?

3 What was the state of domestic abuse before the pandemic of Covid-19?

The police recorded a total of 1,288,018 domestic abuse-related incidents and crimes in England and Wales (excluding Greater Manchester Police) in the twelve months ending in March 2020. Of these, 41 per cent (529,077) were incidents not subsequently recorded as a crime. The remaining 59 per cent

(758,941) were recorded as domestic abuse-related crimes.

4 But crimes of domestic abuse aren't over and done with when the violence or psychological abuse is over. Just as there is Long Covid, there is also Long Domestic Abuse. That's my term for it. For, after the crisis is over and you're still alive, the abuse still enfolds you, imprisons you in the lessons it has taught. That's true for me and dare I say it, it's true for you. Even when you're no longer with the person who has abused you, you may face harassment and stalking.

5 What do official statistics tell us about the incidence of domestic abuse in recent history? Is it rising or falling?

The number of offences flagged as domestic abuse-related has been gradually increasing in recent years (the 2010s). So, it's not possible to determine what impact the coronavirus (Covid-19) pandemic may have had on the increases in 2020.

We have information beyond official crime figures, but the evidence is not conclusive. For example, there was an increase in demand for support for victims of domestic abuse during the Covid pandemic in 2020 and 2021, particularly following the easing of lockdown measures. However, while we don't know for sure whether there was an increase in the number of victims of domestic abuse, the data from agencies that support victims of abuse suggests that experiences of domestic abuse may have intensified during the lockdown.

Moreover, victims of abuse faced additional hurdles in getting support safely under these conditions.

Results from a survey by a Women's Aid provider showed that during the first few months of the pandemic, there was an increase in demand as reported by:

58% of 26 refuge services;

80% of 30 community-based services;

91% of 22 online support services;

and 81% of 31 telephone support services.

These caring agencies expected that demand would increase after lockdown measures eased.

There were increases in demand for helplines between April and June 2020, such as a 65% increase in calls and contacts to the National Domestic Abuse Helpline compared with the first three months of 2020. This does not necessarily indicate an increase in the number of victims of domestic abuse, but perhaps an increase in the severity of abuse, combined with an additional problem. That was how difficult it was for victims to get out and away from their homes to escape the abuse or even to get to counselling.

WHAT'S OUR RESPONSE? YOURS AND MINE?

This modest book attempts two things: a fictionalised account of one man's personal domestic abuse and how it affected him – me - and to suggest ways other victims can resolve their problems. Nothing is more important than your survival. But domestic abuse threatens survival. A core part of our brain fosters the instinct to survive so what I write is relevant to you.

EPISODE 2

Cries: A Beautiful Voice Is Not Enough

Have you ever been with someone too drunk to know what they were doing? No? But maybe you've heard about it from someone who has. When they've told you about it, to get it off their chest, as we say, you've borne the brunt of the story.

You will know there's no point in trying to tell the attacker things he or she can't think through for themselves. So, how on earth do you behave towards someone whom you are so afraid of that you dare not risk provoking them without meaning to?

There's no answer to that.

The night when Red sprayed the flat with glass and for countless nights afterwards, he was disorientated not only by drink but also by his confused emotions. Whatever he might have said, he was tormented inside. He was like a soldier facing certain death who threw himself into battle to wound those whom he loved. It was like the son who has killed his father in William Shakespeare's *Henry VI, Part 3*.

But I can't raise my own tearjerker scenario of domestic abuse and dignify it as some deep tragedy like an Elizabethan play.

***

On this particular Sunday night, crying out every foul

epithet Red could think of when he was gripped by his craze for more bitter destruction, he now seized my bedroom radio. This was a *Wireless for the Blind*, a compact radio that could also play cassette tapes and CDs. It was, and is, a charity handout to bring the sounds of the world to visually impaired people. Red hurled my Wireless for the Blind across the bedroom floor, picked it up and hurled it again until its aerial mast broke off, destroyed.

Later I learnt that this, too, is part of a pattern in domestic abuse. The abuser wants to sever his victim's ability to connect with the outside world. It's about isolation as imprisonment and control - demonic control. Much as I truly loved this radio, I knew that I needed the telephone even more so, whatever crises lay ahead, I had to protect the phone at almost any cost. Without it, I might be lost.

However, fate intervened. Red was now asleep in bed.

I spent the night after Red had banged my radio to bits on the edge of the bed holding onto the bedside table with my right hand as if for dear life.

The damn leaking tap in the kitchen was pulsating with its hideous plink-plop sound. It echoed around the flat. Each drop grew roundly pregnant until it burst on the steel draining board.

I tried to distract myself by thinking constructively about my perilous situation. Constructively? Don't make me laugh. There was a bad taste in my mouth, trailing from my tongue to my throat like a bitter pill that had got stuck and was giving me bad breath. Gross.

I was now so afraid of what Red might do that I began to hate everything physical about him. He certainly had his stupid side, his periodic obsession with fruit machine gambling, his inability to hold onto money, his vain concern for the good opinion of his drinking buddies whose lives were even emptier than his.

As I dozed and dreamed, I heard a long-dead lover from the past telling me all this in no uncertain terms,

"Along comes this asshole and he steals your life, all casual-like. And I don't care if he comes from a broken home."

Red's curdled voice had sounded so evil that night when he first attacked me that I wanted to run away as fast as I could. But I was trapped. Yet I couldn't quieten a question that kept spinning in my head: why don't we act when we know we're in danger from domestic violence?

Well, for one thing, it's a dangerous fallacy that we

are entirely free to act, free to plan ahead.

"Stop this," I told myself, "you mustn't become like Hamlet, delaying and delaying action until it's too late to do anything."

Red was suddenly wide awake again. From his harsh glare, I could tell what he was thinking. I could sense it in his face even if I couldn't see him in the shadows,

"You're trying to turn this situation into a crisis so that you can escape but I won't let you. You need a short sharp shock, a lesson, a refresher course on who runs this joint. It's not you; it's me. You're a slow learner so let me enlighten you - that's one of your favourite words, *enlighten,* isn't it? And who better to give you a revision class than me, Red incarnate? What's more, I'm pleased to teach you. Everything I need is here at my disposal, that's another big word. You know what I mean."

I panicked but I thought help was at hand. All I had to do was pull a cord, press a button on a pendant cord or speed dial a phone number. This was to activate a system the council provided for elderly, disabled or otherwise vulnerable people, vulnerable to their awkward health or unwanted intruders. When you were in danger, you were supposed to alert a call centre who would despatch police or ambulance, or both, to your side, pronto.

That was the theory.

I dialled and a woman's voice boomed out, hearty and jaded. Red was at my shoulder with his hand on my neck.

"Is that you, Blue?" the voice called out. "What's wrong? Are you safe?"

I gurgled out my fear and my despair.

"Is that you, Blue?" the voice called out a second time. "Are you safe? Are you alright?"

I tried again as Red's grip tightened.

"Help me. I'm being attacked," I gasped again.

And the hearty chuckle with the dismissive reply blurted back her vulgar response to others in the call centre.

"I can't understand this shit."

Hurt as I was, it all sounded like Mother Goose in her 18th-century brothel.

"Who gives a fuck?" she gasped. And with that, the helpline phone went dead. Red released his grip and thumped me in the stomach.

"No one likes a grass," he rasped, "not even the old biddies in your precious call centre."

Unexpectedly, he calmed down, got into bed and slept.

In the morning I went through my bits and bobs in the flat piece by piece, setting everything that Red had disturbed the previous night right again, like slotting pictures back into their proper places after cleaning, of which there was also much to do.

The following days were dreary enough.

But I couldn't hide it from myself any longer, when he was still sozzled with drink long after the actual drinking was over, Red saw me as something not quite human. To him, I was a thing that only came alive when what he said was my so-called writing reached a climax, a supposed book written, or pretended page proofs corrected, or alleged e-mails to my editors sent off. That was his opinion. He wouldn't brook any true explanation of the real state of affairs.

When I wasn't absorbed in writing, I became a different person. To Red, I was someone who messed with his head and provoked his inner fears like static electricity breaking up a radio comedy so you couldn't follow the jokes.

Still bruised psychologically by the amused hostility of the helpline sub-professionals towards me, I was pondering my options if any when along came confirmation that I was not alone.

Not long after the council helpline refused to help

me, a pompous councillor came to a meeting of the sensory group. This sensory group was a quasi-informal assembly of the beautiful people, VIPs and relevant council staff who oversaw visually impaired people in Desire. The purpose of the group was to pass information both ways: council plans for VIPs told to the VIPs and VIP problems passed back to council staff.

The fair, flushed councillor who came to our meeting that day looked as if he had come straight out of *Oliver!* - not the novel by Charles Dickens but Lionel Bart's musical. He was all provincial cheerfulness, full of the regalia of his position, not to mention the good capon or other delicacy lining his wobbly tummy. And he had come upon us, the unfortunates, like a Lady Bountiful of whatever sex to regale us with the swiftness, the alertness, the celerity of the contact centre helpline whose staff had dismissed me.

"It's a real bargain to have the communication cord or the speedy dial phone to the contact help centre in your home," he said with smirking self-satisfaction. "They respond immediately to any crisis, medical or criminal. I've just had one put in my mother's house. It gives me peace of mind to know that my darling sweet mother's slightest cry for help, even her very whim for help, gets answered immediately."

"That's not true," I said before he could relax. I wanted to give him a blast of my rhetoric. But I knew I should stay calm because none of the people in the room knew of my misfortunes with Red, neither the details nor my deepening unease. And so, I had to stick to the plain facts, that I had called the contact centre when someone had got into my flat and was pressing on my throat.

"The helpline staff ridiculed me and I was left in an even worse situation than before I had called."

Sensation.

The councillor's plush waistcoat positively rippled with his incomprehension.

Then it was my turn to be surprised. Another VIP, a woman determined to make her point despite any psychological hurdles of shame in having to explain intimate difficulties to people whom she didn't know well, spoke loud and clear,

"I had a fall that led to a TIA. I called the helpline centre. They replied but laughed at my problems with speech. I passed out and fell to the floor. When I came to, I was still on the floor and couldn't move. The receiver of my phone had fallen off the hook. I couldn't get help and lay on the floor for two days until my son, who had keys, came to the flat, found me prostrate and called for an ambulance."

The fat man was stunned. Two cases of helpline dereliction of duty.

Someone else in the room asked pertinently,

"When someone dials the help centre, aren't they meant to send medical help or the police straight away? If someone is seriously ill, like this lady, or being attacked like this old man, [that was me] they can't speak but the speed dial or the cord are meant to signal the help centre to respond straight away."

The fat man from the council fumed incoherently, mopping his brow with a dirty blue handkerchief laced with snot.

"I'm sorry," I said. "But I think the system is a fraud, something simply designed for the entertainment of the call centre staff as they while away their nights, supported by all of us who pay council tax."

The pompous man beat a hasty retreat when our chairman thanked him insincerely for his visit so I didn't get the chance to suggest he should consider his position. I might not have had the courage to do so. But it was how I felt.

A month later and another night when Red rang the intercom buzzer to my flat from downstairs, I could tell he was too drunk to tap in the code, push the front door open, and get himself into the lift unaided. His warlike face on the intercom screen brought back bad memories of his usual lopsided drunkenness, staggering but still ready to fight.

After I helped him into the flat, he barged past me into the kitchen and cried,

"Get out the way, you tub of lard. You're dead as a dormouse."

Then he slammed the kitchen door on my left hand. I felt a sharp, piercing pain. You could say that it gripped me. I couldn't see them properly but I sensed two streams of crimson blood running from my first three fingers. More by instinct than anything practical, I tugged my white hanky from my right trouser pocket and wound it around my left hand.

From the other side of the door, Red chortled, "That got you." But an instant later, he spun his words and tone into self-defence, "It was an accident."

Since I was afraid of what Red would do next, how I had the nerve to answer,

"But it isn't an accident that you're drunk," I don't know.

He wrenched the door open.

"Accident, are you deaf as well as dumb, you old blind cunt? Are you frightened?" he sneered.

"Not yet," I answered with puny defiance like shaking a tiny fist against the incredible hulk.

"But you soon will be."

He spat out these words and followed them with a healthy dollop of spittle aimed at me but which hit the floor.

My handkerchief was now sodden. I took a clean hanky from the tall set of drawers in the bedroom, got to the bathroom, plunged the bloody hanky into the washbasin, ran the cold tap over it and then over my torn left hand. To dry it, I wound the clean hanky over this aching hand.

Red started again.

"Drawers, drawers, funny drawers like a slag's soiled knickers."

He was now in the bedroom. From the hallway, I could see him lug the top drawer out of the tall chest that I had known since boyhood, hold it upside down and throw the odds and ends of hankies, old eyeglasses and their cases around. Then he banged the drawer on a wall, threw it to the ground and stamped on it. The wood was old and cracked easily. The bottom of the drawer splintered and fragmented into shards although three-quarters of the frame stayed intact, a useless U-shape. It was now nothing more than a pitiful reminder of a fond childhood utility.

"That'll sort you out, you fat frump," he said but this time with spluttering incontinence as he wee'd onto the bedroom floor, fell onto the bed and passed out.

I turned the electric heater up. Why? The warmth from the heater was going to encourage Red's drowsiness. The downside was that the heat made the air in the flat musty as if it had been used again and again ad nauseam. Nevertheless, I hoped it would keep Red asleep.

And whilst Red slept, did the years between his long past childhood and his present adulthood melt away so that his memories jostled one another? Did this also happen when he was outside the flat? For example, when he was drunk and fell backwards on a street pavement, did he also fall backwards psychologically through years gone by and think of everything that was wrong with his childhood that still tormented him?

Red's slump into incapacity that night let me get into the kitchen and into a cupboard where there were plasters and bandages. I started to peel the slight protecting papers from the sticking plasters.

Even with your better hand, it's not so easy to bandage the wounded fingers of your damaged hand when they're still bleeding.

After I'd covered the fingers tightly, I washed the sticky blood from the thumb and palm of my sore hand. Then I took a dishcloth to wrap around my fingers above the plasters.

I stopped and lent against the kitchen wall for comfort. This was worse than useless since comfort was there none. I was pathetic. My always variable sight was breaking up. Cubes of yellow and cream replaced firm images of the furniture in my flat. My cheeks were quivering. I was afraid but I was also determined to stay safe. Was Red always going to get me? Was this to be my eternal, infernal fate?

I thought I was going to faint when I banged my injured hand as I went through a door. The new pain was hot as hell and as piercing as a sharp slap across the face in a 3D movie. When I bit my tongue, it drew fresh blood.

My instincts took over. I grabbed a hand towel to mop up the pool of Red's urine on the laminate floor in the bedroom. I took a bigger towel when the first towel wasn't enough. Last, I grabbed a can of Dettol spray to squirt and coat the poor floor with something nicer than addled urine let loose by a wasted drunk.

I edged my way onto the bed. I didn't dare close my eyes in case Red sprang back to obnoxious life and hit me while I dozed. I did wake again. I don't know when. The blood had started to ooze. I moved gingerly, hoisted myself up and edged back into the kitchen for new plasters.

Outside it was raining. As the rain splattered the windows the sound was like woodwinds running up and down music scales on a xylophone.

I sensed Red stirring. I froze. I watched from the kitchen doorway. Without waking, Red moved to the other side of the bed, silently pulled part of the duvet away and then slipped under the duvet and top sheet. Recovering from his binge as he was, he took care to avoid the green iron grill that served as a headboard to our ramshackle bed. That was something I had found on the street.

I went back to the kitchen cabinet. My hand was throbbing unmercifully. This throbbing was just like remorseless toothache caused by an ulcer. The pain was spreading across the whole of my left hand. I felt queasy but I had to pull myself together. My right hand was shaking as if it was sighing. How I got the several double replacement bandages in place on my left hand I don't know. When I turned to go back into the bedroom my wobbly eyesight turned my tiny flat into labyrinths. I was at the dead-end of psychological imprisonment and no mistake.

Back in bed, in troubled dreams, I relived the incident of Red crunching my hand in the door. Of course, I wasn't seeing what had actually happened. The dream showed how disturbed I was as I imagined the several doors from ground level to my third floor flat popping out of their frames and buckling. This was a parody of my psychological fears. "Alternative truth" is how a Donald Trump handmaiden might describe it.

In this garish dream, Red's face was no more than a skull. He looked like a decaying cameo of his late grandfather staring out at me with a malign grin through broken teeth.

Still in the dream, I looked up bleary-eyed, stumbled to the window, wrenched it open and looked out only to see what looked like blood strafing the walls opposite. It wasn't blood, it was the pulsating red light of a police car. It was stroking the other vehicles along our little street.

The rain had become a storm. It woke me as lightning zipped through the sky. Great thunder bursts followed with a harmony of echoes. Then as fast as time moves in a TV soap, the sleepy storm muttered its thunder bursts drowsily in the distance.

***

I should have guessed that more medical problems lay ahead for Red and me.

One terrible night, he fell outside Tricks, a grotty late-night bar.

He had gone there for the birthday bash of one of his drinking buddies. After midnight I went to Tricks to retrieve him. I was not in time. As I turned the corner towards the bar I saw Red, obviously very drunk, fall backwards down five or six stone steps and onto the asphalt street. In a rare moment of silence amid the tawdry revelry, you could hear a thudding crack as Red's head hit the ground.

Through eyes blurring with tears of shock and surprise, Red saw a big hand come down over and above him. It grabbed him by the collar of his shirt. The hand gave a yank and Red was pulled up and off the ground.

The hand belonged to a heavyset doorman, one of the few Red never quarrelled with. Then two revellers went to Red's aid, raised him, and got him, swaying badly, to his feet.

I reclaimed him and with a surprisingly minimal amount of swaying, led him home.

Next day he was off to visit two brothers and a

cousin who shared a house and a Pakistani girl, two towns to the north of Desire.

Three days later he phoned me from a hospital bed.

"I've been ill," Red said, getting straight to the point. And it was a sad and sorry man who continued with what I now recognised was clotted speech. Still in the midst of his crisis, he spoke about it in the past tense.

"My brothers didn't believe me when I said I didn't feel so good. But Vicky, that's Fred's girlfriend, knew something was wrong. The whole of my left side feels like it's frozen, my mouth, my body, my leg, my arm. My bros still thought I was kidding. But a day later I was even less mobile. Vicky believed me. She phoned for an ambulance.

"The doctors said I've had a stroke, paralysed on my left side."

I knew hardly anything about strokes and stroke survivors but I was about to learn.

When I went to the hospital where Red was lying and went to his ward, I found him determinedly playing with his mobile phone, learning how to use it from scratch, like a child beginner, getting his fingers to work the digits as if for the first time.

But in the ward around him, it was a different story. The other stroke survivors were far more incapacitated than Red. From what I could tell in the suffused light of the semi-darkened ward, they were older and shaken by their experience, emotionally as well as physically. Visually, the combination of patients in white, some heavily bandaged, all with pinched faces and some uttering piteous groans as if possessed inside by some spiritual malady, amid a torpid atmosphere of cream beds and curtain-screens, well, the atmosphere was of hysteria bubbling underneath a calm exterior.

My strongest feeling that day was not for Red still in his thirties, but gratitude that, so far, life had spared me such imprisonment of mind and body that these stroke survivors had to endure.

The experienced nurse with the old-school manner who received me was suspicious, even hostile. She came over.

"You're here for Red, aren't you? I tell you straight away that we don't want any more trouble."

"Trouble?" I asked. "How? Who?"

"Some of his relatives, brothers, I think, have been here already. They think this ward is a joke. They think our patients are a joke. They made a game of our patients, sending them up with cruel impersonations of their speech and movements."

I could well believe it. Red had always ridiculed his

uncles and aunts for their coarse jests and his younger brothers and cousins for their pointless lives of petty crime. So, I couldn't say I was surprised by the nurse's words. But she wasn't finished yet.

"Their behaviour was so disruptive that Matron had to come in and tell them off. So, please, no more trouble."

I knew that hospitals no longer had "Matrons" in the way the nurse said and that her term was another warning. I was sober so she moved on with her chores. Outside the ward, a bell dinged softly and a nurse passed the window - we were on a ground floor - and the soles of her shoes squeaked on the concrete ground. I could hear the wind blowing outside. Although it was still summer, it had a cold sound.

I concentrated on Red, encouraging him to use his hands with his phone and walk unsteadily around his bed.

When I returned two days later, the ward was much the same. Cream light from the windows tinged the skin of the patients, making their faces look even more like ghosts. But from his manner, it looked as if Red had improved a little.

"Can you tell?" he crooned as he moved between the beds and the screens.

Indeed, his determination to get his left side moving better was admirable.

I didn't visit him a third time in that hospital, oh no, he came to me.

Early one evening he buzzed the intercom and hoisted himself back into the building, along the hall and up the lift and into the flat. He looked ashen. His face seemed both white and grey at the same time. He was dressed sloppily. It was lucky we were still in summertime when the weather was at least mild if not warm. His eyes stared at me but they didn't see me. They seemed glazed, lifeless as if he was already dead. But he was boiling with rage. His speech was slurred but his words sharp,

"You've not missed me. You've been too busy sleeping around, shopping about for a new lover. Don't try and deny it. I know you, you dirty old man. Nobody gives a fuck for you. But you couldn't wait to put yourself about the moment I was gone."

"What's happened? Why are you here and not still in hospital?"

"Wouldn't you like to know?" he answered, tapping the side of his nose with a crooked finger. "I discharged myself from that piss-pot hell hole. Think you could me hold me there forever? Fat chance."

"I haven't done any of the things you accuse me of. You're ill, seriously ill. You've had a stroke. I can't believe the hospital let you go."

"They didn't. They don't know. They let me go for a smoke in their smoking area, sure enough. I was dressed. I just didn't go back to the ward."

"How did you get here?"

"I came by local train. No one stopped me. No one asked me for a ticket. Here I am and here I stay. Stop you going back to your dirty tricks."

I was at a loss as to what to do. Red watched me attentively as I moved to the sideboard.

"Don't think of getting on the phone. If you do, I'll pull it out of the socket."

"You need help. Medical attention."

"So, that's it. You won't help me, you old fat fuck."

With that he was out of the living room, slamming the front door of the flat, off and away.

Let's be clear on one thing. Whatever Red accused me of, I was not drowning in some endless tide of meaningless affairs.

I locked the front door, picked up the phone and got onto the police straight away. At that time, if you dialled 101 the police would answer the phone and you could explain a crisis that wasn't a crime emergency such as a burglary. I also called the hospital to explain the greater danger Red had put himself in.

Later I dialled the police again. The hospital had now alerted the police but there was no joy. The police had found Red easily enough in the city centre gardens. The policewoman on the phone to me explained,

"The officers questioned Red. His answers were cogent and reasonable. He's an adult. He's of sound mind. He's not in trouble with the law. They let him go on his way. There's nothing else the officers could legally do."

After that, I was left to think things over, not to laugh or cry, just to wait. Nothing I could do, except wait.

Two days later Red phoned again. He was now in a different hospital, some place south of the city centre.

"I got to Chloe's house [Chloe was another of his cousins] the morning after I left you. I'd been out all night. It was pretty early. Chloe and family weren't all out of bed. Rusty [Chloe's husband] opened the door. He saw the state I was in. He got his oldest son, Matthew, to get up and give me his bed so I could lie down.

"I heard Matthew say, 'Why is it always me who has to do everything around here, give up my bed?'

"Rusty told him straight, 'Because home is where they will always take you in, whatever you've done, whatever the problem.'

"Then Rusty had Matt stay with me. Rusty went himself to the doctors, as you know, they're just across the street. The Pakistani doctor came over immediately, saw how I was, called for an ambulance, and they got me booked into the hospital here. Yes, I've been ill. It isn't my fault. Now I'm just tired."

Red rang off. I think he just crashed out. Not only his body but also his nerves were shattered.

I wasn't anxious. I was just in a vacuum of ignorance. Like I said, I didn't know anything about strokes and stroke survivors but I was about to learn, and fast.

There were repercussions following Red's stroke, even when the second hospital released him and he was back in the flat. It took some time before he could walk steadily. His left leg lagged behind his right and he swung it behind his right as if the right was performing a loping pirouette. When he was settled back in the flat, he manoeuvred himself around it by gripping furniture and bookcases.

Now the whole atmosphere of the bedroom belonged to Red: the former hall table, a gilded occasional table with fine legs had become a pitiful dressing table laden with cartons of pills, bottles of pills, and photos of Man United footballers. The bedroom was a true boudoir in the French sense, the place where you went to sulk. And sulk he did.

It also took Red time to hold and manipulate the knife and fork for his evening meal. His compromise to evade embarrassing clumsiness was to spoon all his meals. This led to his choice of meals, concentrating on spicy noodles that only required adding hot water to make a complete but far from a nutritious meal.

ADVICE

Following his stroke, Red was perplexed by invitations to supportive organisations, notably stroke associations. Their meetings were more of a revelation to me than to him. Meetings might be held in hotels with good cuisine such as we could never have afforded ourselves.

Most interesting were the friends and families of stroke survivors. Their questions in debates before panels of experts, and their conversation over lunches besides, had a persistent common theme: how the characters of their loved ones had changed following their strokes.

4 Character Changes after Strokes

1. A mature woman glammed up to the skies, described her plight,

   "My husband used to be so sweet and caring to others, even after a hard day in the office. He was a solicitor. Now, it's not just that he is always grumpy and bad-tempered but, when he asks for help, his words are so hostile and vicious. It's like he's an entirely different person. Sometimes I think I can't take it any more. Yet divorce is out of the question; he's helpless without me."

2. A tired woman with blue hair and a Cockney accent said,

   "Whatever I do for him, it's never enough. My son complains all the time. His speech is blurred except when it comes to ordering me about. He was a skilled toolmaker and ran the local branch of their trade union. Now nothing's good enough for him. We had a stairlift fitted so he could get to the upstairs loo unaided. Once it was working, he didn't want it. It wasn't just that he wouldn't use it, he wanted it taken out. Said it offended his sight. I'm at a loss. I don't think I can cope much longer."

3. A mild man with glasses and low-slung hips explained,

"I owe everything to my mum, everything, not just for bringing me up by herself but for her business acumen. We run a newsagent's shop together. She was always up well before dawn to get the paperboys organised and on their way. I worked for an accountant five days a week so my job in the family business was to keep the books and help out on weekends.

"But it all became too much for mum. She had a stroke. One evening I found her collapsed and gagging in the lounge behind the shop. After her time in hospital, she was too weak to work. Now she sits in her chair all day, staring out the back window. I gave up my day job to run the shop and look after her. But her character is different. She swears like a trooper and complains about every little thing like a sergeant major in the army. It's as if she's had a personality switch in a sci-fi film."

4 Listening to these suppressed cries for help, I got the message loud and clear. The moderator of the stroke survivors' discussion explained it concisely,

"What you're all talking about is the personality disorder that some stroke survivors have. Medics call it cerebral irritation. And I know from my personal life, it's extremely difficult to live with. Maybe the shock of the change, this new character disorder from someone you all loved turning into a tyrant who savours their tyranny of the weak, is one of the most disturbing aspects of the change."

I couldn't, hand on heart, say that Red had had a complete change of personality with his stroke. And in his more reasonable moments he would admit, "I have a short fuse."

However, Red's stroke had shortened his mini fuse into a lightning strike of red-hot anger. Nor would he do anything about it by accepting offers of counselling or any professional advice. That meant when he received the old DLA benefit, he didn't do anything constructive with it.

Benefits of the old DLA

1. Yes, Red was awarded the DLA, the Disability Living Allowance. In the early 2000s, this was a comparatively new benefit, intended to assist disabled people financially to lead lives more on a par with non-disabled people. To get somewhere too awkward for you to travel by public transport such as a hospital that was out of the way; well then, with the DLA you could afford to go by taxi. You could also use it to pay for a carer who might provide personal

services such as washing you and preparing your main meal of the day, or get help in running your home, etc.

2. The DLA had two components: the care component and the mobility component. Red needed much and received both components. We both heaved a sigh of relief but would the DLA help or hinder him on his downward spiral? And what would happen to his famously short fuse?

I also had DLA because of my severe visual impairment - that's the posh way of describing blindness. And, since I was retired I had a pension from work and the regular old-age pension from the DWP. This didn't mean Red and I were well off. Financially, we were in what the government now termed the *precariat,* a new class defined by political leaders in the 2010s. To be frank, our life was a financial struggle.

When either of us got an unexpected bonus, perhaps a surprise back payment from the DWP, we played a weary game of planning our primitive finances, then dividing the unexpected gift into so much money for food, for mortgage and council tax, and, if there was any extra, for clothes.

But in this same period, Red's hot temper could

erupt from misunderstandings or out of nowhere. I was always anxious. When would he hit me next?

RUNNING SORES

In my story so far, you may have discerned some running themes. I call them *running sores* to capture the emotional intensity, the distress they caused me and the nagging aggravation about them that became my constant companion for years.

6 Nagging Fears

In the following six questions and my answers, you can tell I have answered a doubt that had been bubbling away in my brain. What would your answer be to these questions about fear, depression, anger, and confused feelings?

1. Are you afraid to seek help?

    I was anxious because I didn't know where to turn to and how to explain my concerns because the whole situation had left me humiliated and depressed.

2. Was I afraid because I thought I had failed as a partner?

    No, because Red's basic mismanagement of his anger stemmed from his deep unresolved psychological needs.

3 Did I feel angry?

You bet. Along with the fear I was also furious that Red could do and say what he did and I was powerless to remedy the situation.

4 Was I torn by contradictory emotions?

I was conflicted because despite my fears, sometimes Red, my abuser, could be loving and kind, such as when he made sure I got home safely at night in a dangerous part of town; when he insisted on buying a new jacket for me because mine was frayed. And when he cleaned jackets and trousers that had stains.

5 In the maelstrom of physical and emotional danger did I get intensely frustrated because I believed I had tried to make our relationship work by being patient and kind in turn?

Yes, I consistently tried reason and I had failed.

6 Because Red inside was more vulnerable than me, would I feel guilty about a separation?

Yes, I couldn't help myself.

How would you answer the questions above?

4 Different Ways You May be Feeling If You're a Victim

Now, try and step back from the danger you're in if you're a victim of domestic abuse and consider some of the ways you've coped with your problem until now. The following text and argument come from the website of the Commissioner for Domestic Violence, about whom more below.

1 It's a reasonable guess that you've learned to be careful about what you say, when you say it and how you say it.
Living with an abusive partner may make you think it's like walking on eggshells.

2 Have you tried to talk to your partner about their own levels of anxiety, their alcoholism or any drug use, or their dark moods and the stress they put you through?
We victims should never think our partner's violence is our fault. You've tried to make agreements or set boundaries, but this doesn't work when your abuser is off on a bender or gripped by jealousy and suspicion.
Perhaps you've given up trying to persuade them to change because you don't want to say or do anything likely to upset them. In other words, you've adapted your own behaviour to what they say they want.

3 As acts of violence continue and escalate in intensity you may find yourself increasingly gripped by a genuine fear of worse to come. This is that your

violent partner, consciously or even subconsciously, has chosen violence to control you and get their own way in the relationship.

4. Many men don't realise that a partner's violent behaviour to them is domestic violence. They might not have believed until recently that their partner's abusive behaviour could be called violent.

If a man feels scared and unsafe in his partner's presence something is wrong. Yes, some men simply don't want to admit that they are afraid of their partner. This was once a storyline about Tyrone Dobbs in the ITV soap, *Coronation Street*. It doesn't seem masculine for a regular bloke to admit that he lives with someone who is violent to him. It undermines his sense of self-worth. Police officers acknowledge that men probably don't report violence when they should.

You may also sense an unsettling thought simmering at the back of your mind – that the unhealthy relationship between Red and me was linked by a disturbing chain.

We call this: **Co-Dependency**.

This means excessive emotional or psychological reliance on a partner, typically one who requires support on account of an illness or addiction. An official version might refer to this as, "the tie that binds most of us together in this trap called co-dependency."

Another, more academic interpretation taken from Wikipedia on the web declares,

"In sociology, co-dependency is a concept that attempts to characterize imbalanced relationships where one person enables another person's self-destructive tendencies and/or undermines the other person's relationship."

Co-Dependency in Literary Classics

Co-dependency can seem beneficent such as the intertwined relationship between lovelorn hunchback bell-ringer Quasimodo and captivating gypsy Esmeralda in *Notre Dame de Paris* by Victor Hugo. Or it can become destructive such as the *folie à deux* of classic drama's most infamous co-dependent pair, Macbeth and Lady Macbeth in Shakespeare's tragedy. It takes the two of them to conceive and commit royal murder and mayhem.

In Shakespeare's *Othello* there is the unhealthy co-dependency of Moorish general Othello and his nemesis, Iago. Othello represents jealousy and Iago represents envy as Iago programs Othello to kill his innocent wife.

In width beyond depth Friederich von Schiller, German pioneer of the movement we call *Storm and Stress*, gets co-dependency for us wholesale. In his historical epic play, *Don Carlos*, set in the court of Philip II of Spain - and Giuseppe Verdi's opera developed from it - there are no fewer than four co-dependent relationships. If you are curious, the five intertwined characters in the four co-dependent relationships are religious fanatic King Philip II, his son Don Carlos, his third wife, and his bit on the side; then true friend to Philip and Carlos, the unhistorical libertarian Rodrigo. Holding these four in thrall is the fifth, the dreaded Spanish Inquisition. And unlike *Monty Python*, the others are conditioned. They *do* expect the Spanish Inquisition hurtling them to tragedy at a measured pace.

Consider the subject of co-depndency. I bet you can think of your own examples from life and art.

The various points from the commissioner's website bubble away unmerrily through the next episode in my personal account of domestic abuse and how to escape it.

EPISODE 3

Welcome To Hell In Desire

One Saturday evening when I thought Red had settled down to watch *Match of the Day* on BBC1, his temper flared after a Man U player missed a penalty.

Red fired his own shot in his own way.

When the remote he threw hit my cheek, it was like a cold slap across the face. The sound ricocheted around the room like a gunshot.

There was no point in crying. Besides, crying made me look twenty years older and I felt ninety as it was.

Red got up and fumbled on the sideboard for his drink. But he jogged the glass and it fell on the laminate floor and shattered.

"Thanks for being so understanding. Thanks a heap," he said with pretended sarcasm that didn't hide his enormous internal frustration.

I didn't want to believe that things had gone this far. But I couldn't hide it from myself any longer. This was going to be everlasting terror. I was trapped in a life with someone who had turned into a blunt instrument of pain and who was now out of control. There was nothing supernatural about it. I don't think Red ever thought, and far less admitted, that he was doing anything wrong.

He was now ruled by swiftly changing moods from saucy, breezy joy to black, unsettling despair expressed in harsh words that seemed to dance and spit at my impairment with comic derision. As events unfolded, I couldn't help thinking in brief moments of calm how easy it was for him to trash his own life and mine, home, income, comfort, health. That was the truly scary thing. His every action, drinking too much, hitting me too often, it was as if he was deliberately switching on an electric fan and inviting the proverbial shit to fly loose and destroy us both with its gooey brown mess.

I took refuge in the kitchen, a sliver of a room around the corner from the lounge.

"Blue Belle, Bare Bones, get your fat ass out of the kitchen with your kiddies' meals of chicken nuggets!"

Red was shrieking. It was like the persistent echoing yap of a small dog that has never been trained. The piercing sound spread through the flat like a vacuum cleaner out of control, like the alarm bell of a fire engine racing down the street.

I remembered what Red told me that Rusty, his cousin's husband, had said to his son: 'Home is the place where, when you turn up, they have to take you in.'

And this was the first of several times in the scenario of Red's abuse where this turned out to be true.

You could tell what Red was thinking: 'This isn't my real home but it's home in the sense of where I can lay my head down tonight.'

But my idea of home was different. It wasn't any soppy idea that home was a place of comfort and refuge, no, home was the place where you have to face your darkest fears during the blackest night.

As Red's sporadic personal and physical abuse continued over months, there were weeks that remained blank in my memory. I simply couldn't remember what had happened. They were mere spaces between bad dreams and worse nightmares about being attacked.

ADVICE

5 Unexpected Obstacles to Take Your Breath Away

I couldn't give you a coherent account of my attempts to free myself from Red's sporadic rages and increasing violence. But, no matter how embarrassed I was, I now knew I had to seek help, starting with the organisations that were supposed to do just that, help.

1 First on my mental list was the Sensory Team. This was the forum where the pompous fat councillor had misspoken about help for disabled people courtesy of pendant alarms. I started with the head of the Sensory Team.

"I'm sorry," said the team leader after he had listened impatiently to me, "but we never interfere, help, or assist in personal family matters. It's a red line rule with us."

"You mean I'm on my own?" I asked.

"Yep, that's the top and bottom of it. You're on your own. I'm on my own. We're all on our own. Get used to it. That's life."

So our sensory committee chairman had said he would not lift a finger to help me.

2 Next up there was my doctor, Dr Tiz, a rude not so old queen who revelled in malicious put-downs. I was nervous before the appointment. The doctor was late. The muzak played over speakers high on the wall of the pastel-coloured corridor that served as a waiting room was, 'I wish I knew how it would feel to be free,' as sung by Nina Simone. It chimed with my own unsettling blue mood and ratcheted up my anxiety. I feared the worse and it came when the stuck-up doctor deigned to appear.

He was angry because he was late for work but not so angry that he couldn't blast me with his scorn,

"No, we don't get involved in domestic matters like this. You speak to your partner's own doctor. Get him to do the heavy lifting. Just catalogue everything you've told me. He'll find it useful. But we're not going to help you. Now, if you'll excuse me, I have patients to see who are truly ill."

From my perspective, this pathetic little scene between me and the doctor dripped with the unctuousness and spite of a vicious queen made old before his time by unprofessional malice.

Years later I learnt that Dr Tiz's partners had him ousted from the practice for being persistently rude to people. It's a modern axiom that it's okay to be a queen provided you're a nice one. And Dr Tiz failed that test conspicuously.

3. One of Red's assets on which I had relied up to now was that he would occasionally clean the flat, vacuum the laminate and carpeted floors and scour kitchen worktops and bathroom tiles. After his stroke, this was not possible.

Knowing I couldn't see well enough to do all this properly myself and that I needed help with cleaning if I was ever going to manage on my own, my social worker at the time, Dilys Vixen, a pretentious woman with low and behold cleavage, arranged for a cleaning service to come and help me in readiness for ridding myself of Red.

Getting cleaners to come to a downtown flat is no small achievement in a city named Desire where all sorts of workers don't want to drive to, let alone park, downtown.

"You'll have no trouble with us," explained Fred Filch, the smarmy cleaners' manager when he surveyed the flat. "Many of our staff live locally so they walk to work. You don't mind Chinese or black cleaners? No? Good. We have 300 staff on tap."

This was more than a simple exaggeration. It was blatantly untrue. Nevertheless, at first, all went well with the cleaning company. But I began to notice their limitations. The cleaners were fine about admiring and polishing ornaments (which was inessential) but slapdash when it came to core cleaning of floors (which was supposed to be why they had come). In time the company sent invoices for work done, or maybe just claimed for as if it had been done. The invoices cascaded through my letterbox, first a trickle, then an avalanche. I couldn't read the invoices clearly; couldn't specify when this, that or something else had taken place on a specific day. So, I was being overcharged.

Then I noticed other problems. My passport had disappeared from its drawer. And so, too, had my mother's old diamond engagement ring, secreted, or so I thought, in another drawer. When I consulted the company's accounts manager in a phone call, she admitted,

"Something's wrong with the pile of invoices. The cleaners have sent them in way too late. I'll cancel them. But I can't get your ring or your passport back."

Then the smarmy work manager for the cleaning company called to say,

"I'm sorry, we can't find anyone willing to come to the city centre to help clean the flat."

"But you are the manager and you said you had 300 staff available."

"In your dreams."

He meant this to be biting scorn but his curdled voice developed a judder that showed alarm and desperation as if he knew his company was guilty of theft and he just didn't want it to come out. But when all was said and done, the staff had cleaned me out of what few valuables I had and they wanted to move on. Social worker Dilys who had arranged for this mess had also moved out, up and away.

Don't be surprised. Older people and older disabled people, in particular, are easy prey for false-faced cleaners and streetwise rogues.

So, my plan for eliminating my need for Red by finding professional cleaners had blown up in my face.

4 But when it came to personal safety, surely there was always the police? There was not. Police support for vulnerable people may have expired in the wake of wrong-headed financial cuts to social services, courtesy of successive Tory governments reducing funds to local councils, the NHS and the police, to name but three. However, I suspect hard-headed dislike of gays and incomprehension of the basic safety, the domestic and emotional needs of vulnerable people ran all the way through police services.

Let me give two examples:

4a Once again Red had been tottering drunk on the streets and was abusive when he got inside the flat. Verbal abuse turned to fisticuffs when he shoved me onto the bed, managed to twist my arms behind my back and then twisted them individually. He knew this played havoc with my osteoarthritis. I struggled off the bed, got to the phone before Red did and dialled 999.

I was gasping and so incoherent that I don't think my words mattered. The civilian working for the police who answered instinctively understood my distress. She arranged for cops to call round. They were openly hostile and declined help. They surveyed Red sprawled out incontinent on the bed. His condition provided them with the perfect excuse to do nothing. The lead cop with a curled moustache and coiffed black hair, plucked something or other from between his front teeth and said,

"He's high on drugs. That's probably something you know more about than we do. You get him off the drugs and then we'll help you. We're not going to risk ourselves while he's stoned."

"And what about me?" I wondered. "I'm here. I'm not on drugs. What about my safety?"

It seemed the cops could not get out of the flat fast enough, banging the lobby's outer security door as they skedaddled away.

Immediately after the police had gone, I didn't dare cry. But when I jumped into the shower and let the warm water cascade over my shaking body, my eyes blurred more than usual. As splashes sprayed the heavy plastic shower door, it looked as if the door was weeping. That's how distressed I was. I held onto the door handle. I was choking.

I didn't cry a river. I cried a lake of tears and a lake without currents to renew the water.

4b Another time when Red had once again broken glass in various pictures on the wall and glass sprayed around the room, I got to the front door of the flat and out of the security door. I knew Red would follow me so I scampered not downwards but up half a flight of stairs in the main stairwell where I could hide unseen from below. When Red searched the stairwell downwards by stairs and lift and couldn't find me, he assumed I had already got out the front door.

When he went back inside the flat, I moved stealthily downstairs to the front door of the building and made my escape to the police station by the Town Hall.

Let me set the scene there.

There are particular stage sets in my story. When I say *stage sets,* I mean specific environments that we get used to in life. For example, an office you're visiting for an interview, or a supermarket where there are divisions for items grouping together food, cleaning products, etc., for the store's convenience and yours. Simply from your everyday experiences, you get to know how offices are laid out. And you get to know how supermarkets are laid out with their rows of shelves from which you select your purchases. The shelves say, "Buy here"; the food says, "Buy me to Eat me."

Because you know what to expect from offices and supermarkets, you don't have to think about everything anew each time you go to them. Your regular experiences help you negotiate everyday life without having to process everything from scratch every time.

The most regular stage set in any of our stories is our home with its familiar layout. And we get so used to our environments that we have part-created that when we change them, say by renovating a tired kitchen and reordering what's in the new cupboards, we still find ourselves reaching for things the way they were before we changed them.

Sometimes you find yourself in surroundings strange to you.

My first experience of a new stage set in this scenario of domestic abuse was the police station: arid, chairless, with a counter sealed off by windows and a bell to the side. At first, I didn't know what to think. Then the stale atmosphere said to me, "Getting ignored is easy. Getting noticed is much harder, but it is possible. Ring for help. Then we will bury you and your complaint."

Hasn't anything like this ever happened to you in government offices? It sure has happened to me. And this is what followed:

I rang the bell in the police station, waited politely, and tried to stay calm as I stuttered through my troubles with Red.

When he came to interview me, the lead cop was full of himself and his power to administer or withhold justice.

"Do you self-harm?" asked the burly cop as he looked over my scarred hand as if he were in the know and enjoyed putting any gay down. He bent down with an unpleasant smirk as if to underline his put-down question.

I wanted to ask if the police force paid him extra for being too fat to do his job. But I didn't. I really thought I had hit the skids of psychic degradation when this fat bully with the lion's mane beard treated me with such arrant contempt. His sidekick sensed the bully had gone too far but he was too junior to say anything.

Rather than make matters worse with useless explanations and self-justifications, I beat a hasty retreat. That's right. Since I knew I couldn't get help in the actual police station I certainly wouldn't get help in my home.

I wouldn't let the police escort me home.

6 Things the Police Should Do But Haven't

1 When questioning or advising members of the public, police should always state their names clearly and show their badges as proof of identity and authority. In the numerous encounters with police in my story only once did officers tell me their names and show their badges. This should be regular practice not only as a matter of courtesy but also as a precise statement of clear authority.

2 Police should always treat pleas for help with good manners and a sincere show of empathy. It cannot be legally right for police to treat those of us who come to them for help and in a state of anguish with contempt, either in what they say or by dismissive body language or speech, such as snarls of scorn and ridicule.

3 If police give victims of crime instructions as to how they are to proceed and protect themselves, then police should also give themselves precise instructions about following up on crimes. As in many public and private offices, e-mails among police seem to be a smokescreen to cover inaction.

4   Police should record all reported crimes as crimes, not forget about them or erase them from records when inconvenient. And only if police record crimes can any government know what the crime rate is and legislate accordingly.

5   From 2010 onwards it has been all too comfortable for police, along with other cherished national institutions, such as the NHS and the law courts, to blame government cuts for any shortcomings. Yes, government cuts have been wrong-headed, misapplied and damaging to these institutions in the short and the long term.

But police shortcomings detailed in this hybrid book have come about because of bad attitude in not heeding appeals for help and judging victims based on their sexual orientation or their perceived background or history.

In a series of notorious cases beyond this book, police misapprehension led to them ignoring widespread crimes of sex-slave grooming across some northern cities.

Worse, as the murder cases of victims Sarah Everard and the two London sisters, Bibaa Henry and Nicole Smallman, showed, depraved policemen gleefully participated in horrid crimes without scruple or remorse.

6 On the evidence of police inaction to widespread sexual grooming, domestic violence across various sexual orientations, and street violence against vulnerable citizens and children, it is clear that police training should include compulsory subjects of domestic violence, disability rights, sexual attacks and killings. Otherwise, police remain uninformed and directionless.

Met Police Misconduct at Charing Cross

You do not need to take my word for it about police failings generally. In February 2022, a report by the Independent Office for Police Conduct (IOPC), following its Operation Hotton, revealed abuse of police authority in the Metropolitan Police in London. The report, based not on oral testimony or second-hand memories, but police Facebook and What's App messages between 2016 and 2018 revealed there had been a tissue of misogynist, sexist, racist, homophobic attitudinising and domestic abuse among a group of up to 19 officers mainly in the Charing Cross constabulary.

On 2 February 2022 newspapers seemed to explode with lurid details:

One officer had boasted of beating his wife to keep

her in line and for her to come back gagging to him for more abuse and more sex. Officers referred to a colleague as "mcrapey raperson" and a male officer told a female officer that he would "happily rape you." And, "If I was single… I would happily chloroform you."

According to the *Guardian,* another officer advocated sexual violence: "Getting a woman into bed is like spreading butter. It can be done with a bit of effort using a credit card, but it's quicker and easier just to use a knife."

Officers made derogatory remarks about gays, Muslims and disabled people and policemen joked about the Holocaust and killing black children.

There could be no excuse that any of this was locker room banter and even that foul excuse would indicate the scurrilous level of inhumanity to which police had fallen. This report and public reaction to it came as a climax to the tempestuous and scandal-hit management of the Met by its controversial commissioner, Dame Cressida Dick.

According to *The Times,* Priti Patel, the home secretary, and Sadiq Khan, the mayor of London, told the Met to overhaul its toxic culture and raise standards above its totally unacceptable behaviour.

Again, according to *The Guardian*, the Met denied

misogyny was a factor and a spokesperson said: "We do not believe there is a culture of misogyny in the Met. There are a number of recommendations in the report that we will consider before formally replying to the IOPC."

The Guardian concluded, "Of 14 officers investigated, two were sacked for gross misconduct. Misconduct was proven against another two, with one officer receiving a written warning, while another four faced measures to improve their performance."

That was the macro situation.

As my micro story of abuse unfolds, you will see more instances of police inhumanity to man.

Commissioner for Domestic Violence

One character, in fact, a whole category of services intended to help us abused victims is absent from my catalogue of unhelpful officials.

Until I began writing this book, I did not even know there was such an officer as the Commissioner for Domestic Violence. Thinking about it, I might have expected at least one of the officials I spoke to at the height of my terror, whether police, doctor, social workers, leader of the sensory team at my local council, to know about and to direct me to her. But not one of them said anything about her.

On reflection, I see why they, too, might not know about her. The commissioner's office has a very low profile and for visually impaired people like me, an invisible one. The website has no lead or tag or instruction to lead a VIP to an accessible part of her website or any other instruction. Once again, we VIPs are airbrushed out of our own lives.

And yet her first web page is dominated by a huge photo of the commissioner with chic hairstyle and lovely teeth, positively beaming at us. You might laugh for this is a Disneyfication of the office as the commissioner lights up the page with a smile of dazzling monotony as if she were the incarnation of a practically perfect Mary Poppins nanny, a beloved fictional archetype.

The commissioner's photo and by-lines are firmly in the tradition of Hollywood movie posters. A darker interpretation of this inappropriate image is that photo and by-line follow another malign tradition, that of the cult of personality we associate with totalitarian dictators in Central Europe and East Asia in the mid-twentieth century. In such a scenario, we, the plebs, are to be the obedient slave followers of the tabloid photo face. It quite eclipses the important information about what domestic violence is and how to identify and categorise it.

You might think that any victim of domestic violence who follows cheery photos and wordplay will now have no trouble getting help from police, courts and social workers. The commissioner's text that follows presents these apparently ever-present helpers as trusty mates on a continuous walking pavement of progress out of darkness and into light, always smooth and never bumpy. We might expect nothing less from a calculated sideshow to the administration of glad-handing PM Boris Johnson at his most boosterish and beneficent.

But this is far from the reality facing a victim of domestic abuse.

The Chief Problem of Going Public

My catalogue of being dismissed unheeded is not simply about five or six individual representatives of services meant to support citizens. It is about any of us, all of us, who wash our hands out of an awkward situation when it suits us. We do this to evade responsibility. Think of high clerics who have hidden proof of child abuse by priests. Of the rotten pope too afraid to challenge Nazis committing genocide. Of policemen who dismissed complaints by young women of abuse by gangs of predators who happened to be Pakistani. "They" also means you and me. Do we, do you, suffer any remorse afterwards?

You know the answer.

Evasive Excuses

Back to my dilemma with Red. There was an impediment that allowed, no, excused, the police and social services from helping me. For when I first went to them, I didn't have a clear objective in mind besides my need to escape Red's blows and be able to stay in my home. In other words, apart from needing protection, I was inchoate. This means I had only just begun my journey to freedom. I had prised open a closed door yet I still didn't know what legal options there were for me. So, my ideas were hardly formed, let alone amounting to a plan of action.

Police and social services might say I didn't give them exact instructions, which was true. But their response to someone who was obviously distressed should have been better (by the police) and way better than disdainful dismissal (by social services). What police and social services could see was a soul in torment. And they simply didn't know how to respond. Nor did they want to. Whatever their limitations, either of education and understanding or political guidelines, their response should not have been derision.

Or were they really thinking, "He's not made up his mind? He won't go through with it. He's had a lover's tiff, that's all. We'd best stay out of it. Otherwise, we'll be wasting our time."

This brings us to the general dilemmas of victims of domestic abuse. When caught in a torrent of physical or psychological abuse, we victims may think the most difficult decision is to ask for help and thereby go public with our outsize problem. This in itself requires a huge leap of faith and personal confidence.

***

When I was back home after that last contretemps with the cops, Red, flat out asleep on the sofa in the lounge, was none the wiser.

I no longer had any hope for Red or me while I was his prisoner. I knelt down beside the tumbledown collection of mattresses that served as our bed. I hadn't prayed since childhood. Now I began to pray for help:

"Our Father, Who art in Heaven, Hallowed… I don't remember the next bit. Thy kingdom come… on Earth, no, that's not right. When people like me despair it's because we're scared of our abusers. Forgive me my trespasses. You see, I try and pretend my failure to escape is really some sort of compromise, the right thing to do. Must I forgive those - no, Red, who trespasses against me? The social pretence that everything is alright, fine and dandy, keeps me, all of us cornered by domestic abuse, in a never-ending cycle of gloom. It's tragic. Deliver us - me - from evil. Dear God, I've made a mess of this. Forgive me. Someone, anyone, please help me."

I had got nowhere. And now there was more to do. More problems ahead.

***

Red and I faced another shock when our local council removed us both from their list of vulnerable adults to be supported by social workers. I had had a social worker when I was placed on the blind register; Red was assigned a social worker after his stroke. More recently, government cuts to local government finances had resulted in local councils trimming back their budgets on social services so that only disabled people with the most serious impairments remained on social workers' active list.

Worse was to come. The way Red learned that he had been demoted, dismissed, whatever term you care to use, added insult to real injury. Towards the end of one week, I took a call from a woman with an accent that I could only partly understand, asking for Red.

"This is Red Hawk. How can I help you?" he asked the woman politely as if mimicking my phone style when he took the call.

"Can I come and see you next Tuesday morning to discuss your future with us?" she stammered.

"Sure."

"How does eleven o'clock, suit you?"

"Fine," Red answered. His eyes lit up like a cartoon character whose sight has been obliterated by dollar signs. He was thinking of another benefit award.

Came the said Tuesday morning, came a change of plan.

The phone rang at 8.05 that morning. Red was in the bathroom. I was still slumbering but I woke up sharp. A woman's voice declared,

"I'd like to rearrange my meeting today with Red Hawk. Instead of your home, could we meet in the Town Hall? And can we meet at 10 am instead of 11 am?"

There was no point in arguing the toss with that command. But I did ask, "Whereabouts in the Town Hall? It's a big building and in several sections, separate buildings, separate entrances."

The phone went dead momentarily until Red's social worker was prompted by an offstage voice. I hadn't realised until then that social services for children and vulnerable adults, which was the category for Red and me, had their headquarters outside the city centre and not in the Town Hall itself.

"The main entrance to the Town Hall itself," came the social worker's instructions.

When Red reappeared from his bath, he wasn't at all pleased. His sense of direction was so poor that he wouldn't be able to negotiate separate official buildings in the Town Hall square. Yet he went full of confidence beside me. Needless to say, the social worker was not at the main entrance of the Town Hall. I had to think hard and fast. I guessed that she really meant not the main Town Hall but the second council building, the Town Hall extension next door where most of the working offices were located. I left Red at the main entrance of the main Town Hall as specified and went to the entrance of the Town Hall extension next door. The only other person there was a woman of statuesque appearance. She clearly had no idea of which building was which even though she worked for the council.

"Are you waiting for Red Hawk?"

"Yes."

"This isn't the main Town Hall. It's the extension. If you can wait in this lobby where there are chairs and coffee tables but no coffee, I will bring Red to you."

The social worker adjusted her frame in a settee so low that anyone might have a problem getting up from it.

I retrieved Red, introduced the unhappy odd couple and made my excuses to go to a bank, leaving them together.

When I returned from the bank, Red's social worker swept past me out of yet another entrance/exit from the Town Hall extension, stumbled slightly when she saw me and trundled away without an acknowledgement.

Red wasn't incandescent because he was in a big public place with people scurrying hither and thither about their business. But his fury was about to break.

"What happened?" I asked.

"She blew me out. The fat hag. She said they were going to take me off the social workers' list. No explanation. But she didn't know what I was going to do. Or say.

"I told her straight, 'You make an arrangement last week for us to meet at mine; then you change it, calling us on the phone at eight o'clock, order me to meet and you don't even know the fuck where it is we're going to meet. Then you have the bloody cheek to dismiss me like old rubbish because I've had a stroke and my life's worth nothing to you, you old spent hag.'

"I wanted to say much more about this obese waste of space."

"What did she do?"

"She was speechless. Then she said, 'I'm not used to being spoken to like that.' She was nervous all right. Her words of outrage had a sagging beat that juddered.

"'Is that the best you can manage, you old fat trout? You're not even educated. I thought my geography was poor but your inadequacy is in an entirely different league of incompetence. Don't even know what's the Town Hall and what's the Town Hall extension. And the council pays you.'

"'I don't have to take any of this,' she said. I could see her cheeks redden. Not before time.

"As she moved as fast as she could to the nearest exit, I called after her, 'Is that the best you can manage, ducky? Where's your flair and guile to project your deceptively placid phrases about giving up on a disabled person. You missed your calling. Are you off to a job interview at Auschwitz?'

"But she was out the door."

I'm too polite to condone Red for being rude. But I don't condone his social worker's rudeness and cowardice either. Clearly, she changed the venue for the meeting to somewhere where she was supposedly going to be sheltered as well as on top of the situation. And she got more than she bargained for. Given his limited education Red certainly had an insolent mastery of repartee in a crisis, which is what this little scene had been. Later I appreciated that, if the said social worker had made appropriate notes of her contretemps with Red, then the council would have had independent testimony of his rages beside mine to refer to when needed.

As if.

***

When Red received the official DWP letter about the government moving DLA benefit claimants over (or, rather, under) to PIP, Personal Independence Payment, first he looked as if someone malign had dropped a Big Greasy Problem in his lap. Then, for you could see psychological gears shifting inside him, he looked like a guy who was systematically distancing himself from reality, like unplugging internal electrical cords from a microwave one cord at a time, first the black, then the brown and then the yellow and green.

The tangled history of PIP in general and as it applied to Red in particular proved a sombre black comedy, unsettling to anyone who thinks the UK is a free and unfettered democracy.

Over the years governments of different political stripes have tried to decrease funds allotted to disabled people. According to government statistics, disabled people of working age are 20% of the population, higher in certain regions such as the Northwest. You can see that if all disabled people are to receive some benefits, then that is likely to become an enormous sum overall, and, from the perspective of hard-line small government Tories, an almighty drag on the exchequer.

4 Things You Should Know About PIP

1 From 2013 successive Tory governments (in coalition with the Liberal Democrats in 2010-15 and from 2015 solo) conjured up this new benefit, Personal Independence Payment or PIP, to replace the DLA, Disability Living Allowance.

2 There were fine words about this change representing empowerment. But the wide suspicion among disabled people and those who shared their

lives remained that the new PIP introduced with new and more severe requirements for the award had really been invented to eliminate the progressive softening and widening of the DLA by successive challenges in court cases. In fact, to its hidebound critics, the DLA had been defined not by legislation but by successful court cases and a substantial body of case law.

3 Hence, a new law would bring a guillotine down on legal precedents of the old cancelled law. But Personal Independence Payment? Was this really a Personal Independence Grant, making it PIG? Or a Personal Independence Support Scheme, making it PISS?

The head of our sensory team, in a long-time Labour-held council, and the very same man who had declined to help me over Red's domestic abuse, had an even stronger opinion about PIP than mine:

"Whatever Labour politicians say in public or before TV cameras, there's no difference between Labour and the Tories when it comes to disabled people's benefits."

And this straightforward-seeming opinion really was a condemnation of the Labour party. Think about it. If you are disabled yourself or you care for a disabled person, consider its implications. Set it as an equation: Labour = Tories. Unsettling to say the least.

4   PIP was administered not by DWP directly but through a private contractor. The resulting mess provoked a legion of disappointment and outrage. And thereby hangs this next embarrassing episode.

When it came to Red's turn to be assessed for PIP he was summoned to a special unit of the contractor underneath railway arches one town over from Desire.

***

Red was doubly unfortunate. His new doctor had not sent the PIP authority a due medical account of problems caused by his stroke. Because Red's medical records had not been duly passed from one doctor to another and could not be presented immediately before the hearing, he asked for a delay.

Red was told most unkindly by a woman with a shrivelled voice who sounded on the phone as if she were playing a harpy in some amateur dramatic satire, "If you delay or try to delay your PIP hearing you will lose the chance of PIP entirely and receive no award."

On the due day, Red's assessor was a clinically obese

nurse who told us, "My name is Lex Scully. I don't really want to be here. I'm making the best of it. I want to escape to the US to join my fiancée. She's from La Place, in Louisiana not so far from New Orleans. But so far I've failed the qualifying NCLEX exam for our nurses to practice in Canada and the US."

NCLEX is the standard test for nurses trained and working in the UK who want to immigrate state-side. So, Red's interlocutor and failed immigrant nurse was good enough for an independent contractor here but not for the US.

When he examined Red, heavyset and heavy-hearted Nurse Scully went through various questions of mobility, ability to prepare a modest meal, etc.

When the official letter arrived to confirm or deny Red his PIP it claimed Red had scored *nul points* just like a UK entry in the annual fiasco of the Eurovision song contest on BBC1. Red was understandably perturbed: to go from some decent award of the DLA to nothing from PIP at a stroke was beyond his understanding.

Another 7 Things to Know About PIP

1 But there were chances of a reprieve: you could apply for the absurdly titled Mandatory Reconsideration. If you asked for it, an officer of the

PIP determining company would have to explain the reasons for their original decision and present a detailed scoreboard of that decision.

2. When the Mandatory Reconsideration letter arrived, typed on what looked like minimum standard lavatory paper, a bog roll, it was full of gross errors. Which were the most numerous? Typos, spelling errors or errors of facts? The writer had managed to misspell Red's name and devoted most of the letter to a party-political broadcast about the establishment and justification of PIP.

   The shoddy letter was a shocking, self-inflicted indictment of the company appointed to award Red PIP or to deny and humiliate him. But the letter showed that, far from scoring no points, Red had received modest marks in certain areas of mobility and care, just not enough for him to receive the PIP award.

3. With Red's agreement, I wrote a scalding riposte to the incompetent authors of this PIP travesty. All the time I knew that inside him Red blamed me for his misfortune.

   Another possibility was open to Red - challenging the unfair PIP decision and asking for reassessment in court. We held this possibility in reserve, ready to take it, depending on the essential PIP answer to my letter. The second PIP letter could hardly defend inconsistencies and untruths in their first assessment. But, of course, the administrator who replied to me was experienced in dodging clerical bullets. She admitted nothing and promised an internal review, of which we were not to be told the outcome.

This brings me to a basic fact about government compared with private companies.

4. Whatever any criticisms of local government, it will be better than any commercial agency deputed to manage awards and benefits because it will be more impartial since its task is to serve citizens. In comparison, a private company running official business for local government is doing so to make a profit. And what is true of local government is even more true of central government, more impartial still while, again, any private company it appoints to run its affairs exists to make money.

It is simply wrong for any government to carve out its responsibilities, especially on such matters as health and disability, which should be administered by the DWP and not a private company bent on milking the system for its own advantage.

Between Red applying for a court hearing and the

hearing taking place were thirteen months. During this time our local disability rights organisation had found Red someone who completed the necessary forms to press his case, and through him, an advocate within our Town Hall. My name for her was Judith.

Before the court hearing Red's advocate Judith was ill with bronchitis for three weeks. On the day of the court hearing, she was replaced by her office manager, one Trevor who had been born and raised in the same nearby small town as Red.

5   While we waited outside the courtroom, manager Trevor explained to three other applicants (one among his clients and the other two not being represented at all and who had unfortunately placed their trust in Citizens' Advice) that their forms were still incomplete or faulty in some way; that therefore the court could not hear their cases; and that accordingly they should apply for a new court hearing at a later day. So that day three Muslim families left the court empty-handed.

6   I got the distinct impression that Trevor, a lithe dark-haired guy, was an experienced flaneur who got through court appearances on a wing and a prayer.

Red had the right to bar me from his hearing and he

did so, thinking he could impress the three judges better by himself. This proved a mistake. At the hearing, the court members were clearly antagonised that among the arguments for granting Red a PIP award was his alcoholism.

"They didn't say anything," replacement advocate Trevor told me afterwards, "but you could see it in their faces. And there's a widely held prejudice against giving alcoholics state funds.

"It would have been way better if you had been inside the court because Red fumbled. His memory clouded over and he couldn't give precise details of when he had been to the alcohol and drug help centre."

This centre was a stone's throw from Desire's most notorious prison. The morning Red had gone there was memorable only because we found a lovely multicoloured blanket dropped by the roadside. It was sodden but it cleaned up beautifully at home.

Despite Red's awkward court interview, and much to the surprise of Trevor, his Town Hall replacement advocate, the court awarded Red some PIP benefit. Not much but enough to bolster his income and to justify his bus pass, essential for Red to travel locally and nationally by bus and tram.

But consider the new situation many disabled people now faced.

7 You don't need me to tell you that we live lives based on fictions, illusions, comforting or frightening, that we have created to help us steer our way through life's hazards. This was what Jon Hamm's character adman Don Draper thought in the US TV series *Mad Men*.

For many, the solace provided by DLA vanished with PIP. This was not just a loss of money, which many experienced, but also a loss of status, absurd though this might seem.

***

When Red came out of his disturbed reveries about PIP, as I said, he didn't blame the government for the enforced journey of self-justification it was imposing on benefit beneficiaries. Oh, no, he blamed me. His mistaken belief got compounded when the DWP reduced his ESA award on the grounds that he didn't need the full amount because I was supporting him. Logically, you might think that if government reduces a claimant's money because they are being supported by family or partners, government should pay family or partners for their support. This, of course, is not the way the system works.

To Red, government shift of policy from the DLA was somehow all my fault. He went into a spiral of denial. And he would make me pay for his new misfortune.

Red's drunkenness and his violent rages were his constant companions over years. Mine, too, for I felt the brunt of them, like Jane Austen's Mr Bennet with Mrs Bennet's nerves.

There was a third, more terrifying companion for Red than the others, gout. In Red's case, gout began with painful swelling of his knees, most biting when it erupted with internal crystal-like lacerations under the skin. It spread to his feet. I think gout in the feet feels like you're walking on glass splinters. But the glass is inside your foot, not on the ground beneath your feet.

There were remedies, medications, to decrease swellings and to lessen the pain. Red concocted a topsy-turvy explanation that "When I lay off booze, my gout is harsher than -"

"When you simply drink your life away," I concluded, quite daringly.

Of course, I don't *know* if Red's explanation was true or not but gout played havoc with his temper. However, it was also so painful that it sapped his violence.

Among famous historical victims of gout PM William Pitt the younger may have had the excuse that excessive port drinking eased his internal psychological conflicts during the almost interminable Napoleonic wars. But Red didn't have the excuse that he was leading a country through war. Red was just at war with himself and doing nothing to stem his alcoholic vice.

***

When he awoke on the sofa that night when I had failed yet again to get help from the police, Red was in terrible pain. It was as if his gout had come back to lecture him:

"Ready Red? Yes, it's me, I'm back, your uber-friendly Gout, the great gift that the unfeeling, uncaring Universe has bestowed upon you. Let me explain it carefully so that there's no doubt, no misunderstanding. This time, perhaps the pain I'm causing you might just be enough to finish you off! Wouldn't that be just wonderful? Better than any super-orgasm? I'll say."

Red's friendly gout increased his exasperation with life.

Don't for a moment think Red's blustering mix of coercive control and sporadic violence was confined to our home. His obsession with me and his jealous fear of betrayal spilt out across our neighbourhood.

The most bitter incident engulfed an innocent staff member at the gym where I worked out. The gym was just around the corner.

While I was out Red would open up my PC and trawl through the e-mails, scouring contents for proof of my imagined infidelities. One evening Red came across an innocuous note from Jim Johnson of the gym.

Sandy-haired Jim had turned his health and his life around from compulsive eating and drinking when he worked in business to committed exercise and diet as a loyal staff member at the gym. His e-mail simply read, "Keep up the good work of your training schedule."

The site Jim sent the message from was Hot Mail.

When I returned from an evening doctor's appointment, Red responded to Jim's e-mail with fury redoubled by heavy drinking:

"Caught you out this time, sure enough. Hot Mail is a well-known gay dating site. You dirty bastard. I'll have you and your new toy boy."

"Hot Mail isn't a gay dating site, it's a connecting platform like BT internet, which is what we have here," I said weakly.

"You can't fool me. It's for dirty old men. Just you wait. I'll get round to the queers' gym and shout the odds."

Like I said, there was no reasoning with Red when he was off on one of his tirades.

I picked up the bag I had momentarily dumped on an armchair. As I turned around, I saw Red was leaning over me. He had broken the top of a Moroccan ornament of a racing horse. He was surveying it. Its jagged neck was so close to my face. I felt him graze my face slightly as I froze motionless to avoid greater pain.

"You've always said your face was never your fortune. Don't you think we could improve it with plastic surgery? Not glass or mirror as our tool but this Moroccan bark wood, fair wood to ugly face flesh. How does that strike you?

"Tell me whom you've been sleeping with at the gym and I'll postpone the pleasure of plastic surgery without the inconvenience of anaesthetic. That way you get to keep the snot burping out of your squat nose. I get my answer and off I go to the bastard in the gym to exact my revenge. Nice. When I'm mad with justifiable anger, time goes so much faster. It simply whizzes by, don't you think?"

"Whatever you do to my face, I won't give you the name of an innocent man. I've done nothing wrong, nor has he."

"So, there is a he, then?"

"No, that's not what I said."

This was all I could expect from the tiresome, tedious, ineffectual man with whom I had to cope. What had happened to us? I felt as if some tired old dinosaur had picked my insides clean. It was like I had been emptied of my emotions. Red had been steadily sapping them until I was hollowed out, empty.

Had I gone along with him to the gym his behaviour would have been even worse, giving him two audiences to play for, the gym crew and me. But I did phone ahead to warn the gym staff.

"I'm sorry. My room mate has gone off on a bender. He's very drunk. If he turns up and causes trouble, call the police straight away."

My call was too little and too late. Red had already stormed his way into the gym and was calling the odds, striking all his usual livid notes,

"I wanna speak to your Jim Johnson, queer as a three-dollar bill. Get him here straight away. He's been having it off with my boyfriend, sending dirty messages on the web. You get him the hell here straight away. I'll sort him out proper, see if I don't."

Neither the fair young receptionist with the indeterminate fascinating accent nor the fey but firm duty manager was nonplussed. Had they heard similar tirades before? After all, our neighbourhood was sprinkled with pubs, way more than doctors' surgeries, churches and restaurants, and far more than schools, of which there was none. So, an occasional drunk fest and more than occasional steroid abuse were certainly a recognised liability in a city centre gym.

Reading this, you may think I was a coward, but, remember, each time I had called the police about Red's behaviour or violence, I had been brushed aside. What saved this horrible gym scene from escalating that evening was the sincere incomprehension of the staff and something else. Having entered the gym blasting away at full volume, and having met with genuine incomprehension, Red's outrage had nowhere to go. Since the gym was on four levels and Red didn't know its layout, he had no way of causing calculated damage without injuring himself. Drunk as he was, he must have had an inkling that his outrage had nowhere to go and he beat a tactless retreat.

That was not the end of the story. While the duty manager and the receptionist said they accepted my apology, we are talking about a gym on the edge of a gay community with all its malice and guile. The axe of the gym's resentment did not fall on me because I was a paying customer. It fell on employee Jim Johnson who was entirely innocent.

On the pretext of protecting him from the senior manager, poor Jim was hauled before a self-appointed committee of moral worthies including the smarmy head receptionist and the unctuous fitness manager. They had no choice but to accept Jim Johnson's sincere incredulity about the bizarre scene because the fault lay with Red and me. However, their interest was prurient.

"Have you slept with Blue Sirocco? Have you had sex with him?"

These questions were asked and denied as if the worst thing that could happen to anyone in Desire was to sleep with me, apparently a fate worse than death and clearly punishable by getting you fired.

Later when Jim first saw me in the gym he responded with a very distant hello. But after a while, he came up to me when I was exercising on the chest press. He wanted to reprove me,

"I did nothing. All I did was be pleasant and agreeable to you. They asked me if I was sleeping with you. They are my friends. They saved me from the senior manager. From now on, I'm gonna be distant with all gym members. And, another thing, how could you let someone like that into your life?"

You won't be surprised that, whatever face I showed

to the world, inside I felt worse than ever.

And I hadn't wondered how the crisis with Red Hawk had got so bad. I knew the answer: I had exposed myself, so to speak, and the danger I was in, to all the agencies you might expect to help me. And every one of them, my doctor, the police, the city council sensory team, my social worker, had turned me away. And they had one common way of doing it: ridicule.

History, in general, is full of what-might-have-been and what-should-have-been. And this doesn't just apply to political history or social history but your personal history as well as mine. So I'm not blaming myself for not having thought everything through as well as I can now with more experience behind me. You might say that I had let myself down. But then you would have to consider that that was part of Red's coercive control over me. Such control was and still is a cornerstone of the general pattern of domestic abuse.

Incidentally, not long after the mini-crisis, the butch-seeming fitness manager took himself off to a more lucrative job at the regional airport: baggage control.

***

Have you ever spent an unfortunate Christmas when a sudden adverse event plunged the entire holiday from glee to despair? No? Well, you must have seen Christmas Day episodes of a TV soap on BBC or ITV where a psychological explosion bursts at the dinner table; something secret and harmful that has been simmering away for months, known to the audience but not to all the soap characters, and building fitfully to its climax.

Well, something like that sure happened to me, caused not by Red's malice but his recklessness. Do I really mean that?

One dry Christmas Day I went to the brief spoken Matins service in church before returning home for a supposedly quiet uneventful day with Red and a modest meal. He was to have ham; I was to have turkey without all the trimmings.

While I was setting everything up, the intercom buzzer ran.

"Hi!" said the voice at the front door of the building. Dimly on the monitor, I recognised the face. It was CR, a middle-aged man who had an actor's equity card but could never find professional work as an actor. He earned his living skivvying for older people. Life had dealt CR a bad hand – what with his lack of money and lack of charm. His problems were made worse by his needling way of trying to touch you up when he was drinking. That hardly compensated.

I was surprised to see CR but I let him in.

When he got to the flat, he offered me an old CD compilation album of popular classics. He was a little out of breath having walked from a suburb three or four miles away.

"I thought you might like the CD collection and could play it as background music for your other guests."

Other guests? What was this?

As we chatted nonsense, *betise* as the French would say, it dawned on me that CR had thought he was coming to a Christmas party, a get-together of other friends who might otherwise be alone for Christmas.

When we had a brief moment to ourselves in the bedroom, I asked Red,

"What is this? CR thinks he's coming to some Christmas party. I don't understand. I haven't asked him here."

"No," said Red. "But I did. He was in the Glass House yesterday on Christmas Eve. I felt sorry for him. So I asked him here."

"You asked him here? He thinks there's a party. But we're on our own. And you didn't tell me. I don't even have food for him. You didn't want turkey. You don't like it. So, all I can offer him is a prepared turkey meal from meals-on-wheels for oldies like me."

Red smirked in a creepy way, trying to conceal that he had landed us in duck soup. He wasn't going to apologise or help.

"You can't hurt his feelings by telling him there's no one else. No party."

While I was wondering how I could entertain, let alone feed CR, I said to him,

"We live very simply here. But I do have a turkey supper if you would like. It comes from meals-on-wheels."

"You bet. Turkey supper is one of the grander meals-on-wheels offerings that my older clients in my day job talk about."

"I don't think *grand* is such an apt word here but see what you think."

CR tucked into the meal, saying,

"You know my clients always criticise meals-on-wheels. They complain about everything, the size of the portion, how the meal has been put together. But I think this is really good, scrumptious in places."

"Like the curate's egg," I thought. But all I said winsomely was, "That's good."

Red now started his menu of the day, cutting me up verbally with his knife and fork tongue.

"Blue thinks this Christmas is just a bad dream and he's gonna wake up. Well, Blue Belle, let me tell you this loud and clear when you do wake up on Boxing Day, you're going to wake up in the hell of your own guilty conscience for all your putting yourself about, not that anyone's even interested."

Since I was with company in my own home, I resisted, answering back, "You've got this all wrong, Red. And don't even think of twisting things round to get the guest."

"Come, come you two," said the unwanted CR. "Stop quarrelling. It's Christmas."

I thought I would hit the roof but of course, CR was an innocent victim. Red was playing his own version, not of get the guest but of get the host and his wrangling simmered through a forlorn day.

I heaved a huge sigh of relief when CR left in the evening for Tricks, one of the few local bars to open on the evening of Christmas Day.

Red subsided into sullen silence. His only memorable comment during, as expected, an explosive episode of BBC soap *EastEnders*, was to say about a situation with a threatening character holding his temper in reserve against someone else,

"He's going to make her life hell," a comment that of

course applied more to him and me than any frazzled screen blonde.

We sank into morose silence glad as night drew on that midnight would soon bury Christmas for another year. But instead of chimes at midnight, the intercom buzzer ran.

CR's blurred voice said, "Let me in."

I was truly astonished but I shouldn't have been, just wishful thinking on my part. It was a very sorry CR who appeared in the flat doorway. He had a large white patch on his forehead and a hangdog expression on his face. I was too surprised to say anything but I didn't need to.

"I went to Tricks and got everyone dancing."

I knew this was stretching the truth since Tricks was a nightclub where people drank, smoked, sniffed poppers and did whatever else.

"Anyway," CR continued, "the club is on different levels. Someone tripped into me and I fell and my head got gashed. They've given me first aid and bandaged the cut."

Red gently eased CR into his sofa, moved his legs around and steadied his feet on a sidearm. And CR fell asleep at once - passed out.

In the bedroom, I told Red, "But I don't want him here. I never asked him."

Red said, "It's obvious he's drunk. Well, you know more about that than I do. There are no buses until seven or eight in the morning. There's no transport. He's in no state to walk home three miles. Let him sleep it off."

And, with that, we retired. I suppose the good thing was that with such a forlorn guest in the flat, Red had to behave and not pick another quarrel with me.

Come morning, CR was still asleep at eight o'clock, nine o'clock, ten o'clock and only roused himself and his hangover at noon.

"Would you like us to go with you to the hospital?" I asked more out of politeness than genuine concern.

"I'll manage. I'll be okay."

With Red guiding him down the lift and out the front door, CR trundled himself off, no wiser, and still, presumably, blaming us for his spoiled Christmas Day.

**

In the welter of physical abuse, I should have taken more notice of another of Red's weapons of choice, his urine.

I certainly noted when he had had too much to drink and was away from pubs where there were toilets, he would find somewhere nearby to urinate, a dark side street or a slice of wasteland where there were dustbins.

He had his favourites. Near the building we lived in stood an old telephone box, directly opposite a bank, later closed. When he could not hold his urine in or when he feared it cascading through his jeans, he would enter the box as surreptitiously as possible, given that it was also at a major road intersection with traffic lights, let himself go and then try and exit the box as if nothing was amiss.

Later I had another clue about his urine. He had come home during daylight hours and, desperate for relief, let himself go over the green-tiled Victorian vestibule just inside our main front door. I was not there. But when he got upstairs inside our flat and was trying to sober up, he told me what he had done.

"I have to tell you because another tenant came in, a girl. She saw me do it and rushed past me, obviously agitated."

No sooner had Red finished his brief tale when the phone rang.

"This is Brad from two floors down. My next-door neighbour is Chantelle. She's just seen Red pissing inside our building all over the hall. She's very upset, frightened."

"I'll have to look," I said curtly.

I looked all over the hall on our floor, up and down some of the stairs and right through the downstairs hall from the lift to the front door. There was no sign of urine anywhere on carpets, hall flooring, steps. Nothing. I didn't know if Red or the girl had made a mistake about where he had urinated, which was why I looked in different places.

Holding my temper in check I phoned aforementioned troublemaker Brad back.

"I've looked up and down the hall, vestibule, stairways and so on. There's no sign that anyone has urinated."

He said, "I've looked too. I guess someone may have cleared it up."

"There hasn't been time."

This ended the conversation but not my irritation at both Red and his accuser.

After his verbal assault on gym staff and the alleged urine shower, Red calmed down for a while. This gave me some breathing space to reflect on my safety or the lack of it. If it wasn't outright domestic abuse, like my battered fingers or thumps below the belt, it was a slow-slow drip of relentless questioning, wearing me down in some sort of psychological pit. How could I escape?

ADVICE

3 Negative Attitudes to Ignore

1. I've heard some people, audience members at a play or a show, so sure of their facts say confidently after seeing a scene of domestic violence on stage, "I wouldn't stand for it. Forcing sex on someone is gross. Hitting someone is perverse. I would get rid of him and no mistake. I would call the police. If that didn't work, I would simply leave."

   And go where exactly?

   They wouldn't put up with domestic abuse and no one else should either. They have spoken; indeed, they have opined. And we have all heard their message loud and clear. But unfortunately, they have decided about something they don't fully understand and don't want to. You see, there is an unspoken assumption in their dismissive attitude that victims of abuse are partly to blame. In other words, we victims have allowed, enabled and encouraged abuse.

2. This typical reaction is a classic instance of what analysts call confirmation bias.

   This harsh confirmation bias comes from people unwilling to accept beliefs, arguments, or ideas that run counter to their core views. So, in trying to convince such people, as well as you, what I need to do is get them to leap over the hurdle of their bias.

It's certainly true that there are myths around domestic violence. It's worth noting that the facts about family violence are often distorted.

In a guide for journalists, areyouok.org.nz provides some interesting insights, which, courtesy of the commissioner, include the following myth-busters:

It's an unpredictable private tragedy.

A Not true. The victim will almost always have suffered violence for a long time. And that was my experience as minor abuse turned into a crescendo over ten years.

B Family violence is almost always a series of tactics used to gain and keep control. It's a pattern of behaviour that increases in frequency and severity over time. Murder is the extreme result. And we know that most such murders happen following the most dangerous time for a victim - after separation.

C Not all family violence is physical. Psychological and emotional abuse don't leave cuts and bruises and broken bones. But its unseen, emotional damage can be as great and the effects as long-lasting.

Psychological abuse can be caused by repeated put-downs and name-calling as well as intimidation and harassment that make us victims feel bad about ourselves.

This was my experience. Red frequently ridiculed me in public or compromised me by bad behaviour such as losing his temper in the audience in the Royal Albert Hall while at the same time telling me that it was me who was doing this to him. He would say, "You make me feel so small."

But fear lurks within the stale convictions of people who judge us harshly. For when they ignore or blot out information and ideas that challenge their long-held convictions, it's because they get upset at the very notion that their comfortable world picture may be inaccurate or faulty.

Of course, we need our core assumptions about society, about the world, about politics, art and religion. Without them, we would have to always be revising our own mental shorthand by which we understand the world around us. This includes such seemingly trivial but essential matters as how we arrange our kitchens or living rooms (as I've said before) and, on a wider social level, how we arrange our regular commutes to work (or not).

For we shape our world in our own image. And to be challenging, even revising it, every day would be overwhelming and exhausting.

3   In recent times among the most successful, indeed arch, manipulators of people's core assumptions, and always in their own interests, are Donald Trump and Boris Johnson, and the Taliban desperado generals. Master copy writer Steve Harrison in *How to Write Better Copy* (2016) suggests why.

Donald Trump before, during, and after he was US President appealed to wide swathes of people who thought the American political establishment had left them behind. They hoped that Donald Trump would be their champion, reviving an outdated isolationist cry from the early 1940s of America First!

The original America First, cooked up at Yale University in 1940 with a fine poster boy in then student Kingman Brewster (who later became a Yale president), had a self-serving mission to keep the nation and its boys out of World War II.

Years later, the old two-word slogan *America First* appealed to uber patriot Trump. As an adroit manipulator via an onslaught of tweets, Trump even convinced his devoted supporters that there were alternative truths, most outrageously that the 2020 presidential election that he lost was in fact stolen from him by a corrupt swamp-soaked Washington hierarchy.

As a candidate for president, president in office, and defending champion, Trump harnessed millions of people's real needs by playing on insecurities within their confirmation bias.

UK PM Boris Johnson was himself a tool of another's superior political skill. Committed Brexiteer adviser Dominic Cummings deployed Boris Johnson's cultivated hail-fellow-well-met bluff persona to convince Brexiteers at large that the UK paid the EU £350 million per week that would be better spent on our National Health. And then, that electing BJ would get the seemingly never-ending Brexit saga finished. Brexit would be done and dusted.

Once again Johnson and Cummings played upon the justified anger of their electoral base over delays in attaining Brexit, stoked by decades of press outrage at EU wastages. The entire sorry Brexit saga proved to be a cornucopia of confirmation bias among both Brexiteers and Remainers.

As to the Taliban [the militant insurgents who regained Afghanistan in 2021], there was what is over-politely termed a cognitive dissonance between what the words of its political trimmer diplomats said to mass media about the rights of women and girls when discussing their intentions during their military campaign, compared with the prescriptive actions of the desperado militants in charge of its siege armies. Both played on stereotypes within and without the teachings of Islam. But the brutality of Taliban actions removed the inconvenience of independent political thought.

The previous eight paragraphs are more than a digression. They show different means by which master political puppeteers manipulate confirmation bias for their own interests.

These examples are outside the subject of domestic abuse. But the subject of domestic abuse in political discussion has more than its fair share of the misuses of political bias.

4 Breakthrough Ways to Combat Domestic Abuse

1 There is, however, such a thing as genuine alternative truth for people who do see things differently. It is a core principle of communications theory that the meaning of any message, however it is conveyed, whether by print, spoken word, electronic media or any other way including how we dress, depends on how it is received. And reception depends on our individual minds and mindsets determined by class,

income, socio-economic group and a host of variable factors.

Returning to the tangent about manipulation:

Donald Trump and Boris Johnson instinctively understood how it is reception that interprets meaning; Dominic Cummings appreciated it intellectually. The Taliban used it to bludgeon an entire region.

2. A regular example of how different people see and interpret things differently is how various are our different responses to the same performance of a play, a film, a concert or a TV program. At its worst are pernicious instances of disinformation about vaccines to protect us from Covid-19. Some people have died because they declined offers of vaccination.

What has any of this to do with you?

Most of us are in the category of manipulated. But we can see the difficulties as hurdles that can be overcome.

3. So, you realise you're the victim of domestic abuse or that your friend, lover or family member is such a victim. That's the first breakthrough step. It may have been a long time coming but at least you accept the fact. The likelihood is that, with the realisation that

you or your significant friend is being abused, you will feel instinctively that you or they must get out, escape.

No matter how difficult the obstacles are, you do have options for yourself and your abused friend or family member.

4 To guide you, I'm telling my story. I trust that you empathize with me and my sorry plight. The core of the story is what happened to me, chronic domestic violence, both physical and psychological. That was the problem.

But although I was a lead character in this story, the hero of the book and a way to resolve the core problem is you; yes, you the reader. Together, let's go on a journey to see how I resolved my plight and, by implication, how any of your family or friends can do so too.

Is this classic storytelling? You decide. For if I, to repeat myself, became a victim who wouldn't go away, you are the hero as you acquire the knowledge and suggestions in the book.

5 If you realise that you are the target of domestic abuse, you may think your only way out is physical escape.

If so, I know what you're thinking. What will your

family think? What will your friends and neighbours say?

Before you worry about that, let's be practical. Do you have friends or family nearby? Do they have room for you? If you've been battered or bruised, would they be able to care for you? Would they want to saddle themselves with you? Would they fear your attacker as much as you do? And, whether you're on your own or with family or friends, do you have funds, enough money to survive?

6 Do you have children? Then your problems of escape are more complicated. Are you going to leave the kids behind or try and take them with you? Can you make a run for it from the big bad wolf with your kiddies in tow? And will the big bad wolf track you down and blow the cover of your new refuge, then blow down that home with you and your kids in it?

7 Now we come to those undermining psychological questions. What will your family think? What will your friends and neighbours say?

Ignore your doubts for the time being. Put them out of your mind.

Yes, there may be some of you who are still fearful of what your neighbours or family members will say.

Will they take your side? Will they say the breakdown was your fault, that you couldn't manage? Will they judge you? Would they think you let the family down, your own family? Or, worse still, will they declare they have to be neutral as if violence against you and legal arguments for your abuser are evenly balanced on the scales of justice?

Is that what holds you back from your escape to freedom?

8   Then, as I keep mentioning, what about the agents specifically appointed to help you? The police? Any council-appointed guardians of vulnerable adults and children?

Have you ever seen one of those shock horror movies when a victim is held hostage by a deranged gaoler? It's a staple plot of pulp entertainment. Think of faded star Joan Crawford, now wheelchair-bound - and she isn't a wheelchair chooser - held hostage by lunatic sister Bette Davis in *Whatever Happened to Baby Jane* (1962).

Think of lovely Samantha Eggar held captive by obsessed butterfly aficionado Terence Stamp in *The Collector* (1965). Or injured writer James Caan in *Misery* (1990) captured and tortured to produce the "right" ending to his novel by sadistic uber-fan Kathy

Bates who also insists he cleans up his fictional characters' language. Which is the worst moment? When La Bates breaks poor James Caan's legs or when she forces him to burn his cherished manuscript?

Now, back to you.

9 Whatever your gender, whatever your sexual orientation, what is holding you back from escaping your attacker? That's how the authorities see it: "Victims everywhere, pull up your socks and don't be a wimp."

So there. And to repeat myself, (it's my only fault), what's holding you back?

Is it something moving to the front of your mind that we might drool over and call love? Is something telling you that you are in a love relationship or emotional dependency, even if love has died? From being a lover, your partner, well has he or she become a situation? Or are you still young and tied to your attacker by sexual feelings? Some might term it lust.

In these different feelings of attachment, emotional, sexual, comforting or whatever, you have this nagging doubt that your naysayers are right, that everything that has gone wrong *is* somehow your fault, that you are the guilty one even when it is you who are being attacked.

Your partner may have a brilliant mind or he or she may not be the sharpest tool in the box but, quite consciously, they are programming you to make you think, or even worse, to believe, that everything that is going wrong *is* your fault. This is what the characters played so memorably by Bette Davis, Terence Stamp and Kathy Bates tried to do.

In other words, you're being made to think you haven't planned things better; you've been inconsiderate or selfish. In reality, it's the other way round. The programming to make you doubt the evidence of your own fears is part of your abuser's brainwashing that coats domestic abuse with your unnecessary feelings of guilt.

Take the example of mother and daughter in Rodgers and Hammerstein's timeless musical, *Carousel* (Broadway 1945; first movie 1956). Billy Bigelow, the wife-beating husband and then ghost father strikes out when he feels inadequate yet his daughter believes that, when you love someone, it doesn't hurt when they hit you.

This is fiction and glorious entertainment. But in real life hitting hurts.

***

Despite all the hurdles, do you still plan to escape? Well, as supreme lyricist Stephen Sondheim puts it, "Maybe next year."

I should talk. I was more like Hamlet than anyone you may know, questioning things, delaying things until it was almost too late to do anything.

So far, and it was very far, I had drawn a blank. After the contemptuous way the fat bearded policeman with the ridiculing snarl had dismissed my plea for protection against Red, I thought, "Well, that's that. Social services won't help me. The police won't take me seriously. It really is my fault. I've allowed myself to be trapped into a corner of humiliation, a dreary hole of everlasting contempt punctuated by sporadic violence."

That's what I thought. What I muttered under my breath was,

"My eyesight isn't going to get better. Quite the reverse. Don't worry. I'm not even thinking of killing myself. I'm just going to have to make the best of it."

So, my New Year's resolution was: "Try to deal with whatever happens." New Year's resolution? Peel me a grape. It was always a New Year's resolution; last year, this year and endless years to come. Even the resolution was its own special sort of remorseless trap.

Until then I hadn't heard the song, "I will survive." But when I did it sure struck a chord that resonated through me. I was nursing a glass of red wine in the Glass House and minding my own business. Then the jukebox started up.

I didn't know then who this singer was but, when she let rip, she had vaulting phrases that seemed to spin around the bar.

You may think this unbelievable, that not until the 2010s had I ever heard a song of 1978 written principally by Dino Fekaris and forever associated with Studio 54 in New York and disco beat more generally.

In this, her best known and loved recording, Gloria Gaynor showed she had a rare gift of expressing inner feelings within a song. And singing and song drew me up sharp; notably the lines about no longer being a chained up little person.

Not that I was ever petrified by Red's absences or lost without him by my side. But I had often been petrified by his violence and no mistake. And Gloria Gaynor implied some of this with such bite that she made us, her everlasting audience (courtesy of recording), think we were listening to something private and deeply felt.

The crucial message, "I will survive," seemed literally chilled out of a wrenching experience. Yet Gloria Gaynor belted out her deepest statement breezily as if there were no tomorrow. And rather than reaching an even breezier climax, the final fadeout notes of the song were steeped in pathos.

But how was I to use the energy this insidious song had given me with its emotive metaphorical kick up the ass?

Then something unexpected did happen to set the cat among the pigeons.

EPISODE 4

Crises

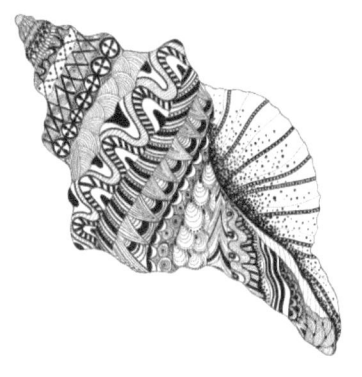

Over four years there had been sporadic leaks into my third floor flat from the bathroom of the flat above. Sporadic because the cause was a floorboard being held in place not by a nail but by a screw banged into it. When it was warm, the screw shrank a tiny bit and water dribbled through the upstairs floorboards, down through my ceiling and farther, across and down my walls. I was never able to remonstrate with the upstairs landlord who always evaded my phone calls and the property managers of the building wouldn't help.

They could teach the police a thing or two about contemptuous dismissal.

But when a water tank on the same dreaded fourth floor opened its bowels and the water spread this way and that, affecting different flats and common areas, inner and outer lobbies, extinguishing lights and spreading its filthy charm of brown effluent, the management company had to take action. They persuaded our insurance company to agree to remedy the multiple problems. In my flat not only were there horrible brown stains on the ceiling and walls in four rooms but also, in the kitchen, damaged floorboards soaked to the skin. And they had risen. That's the technical term for when floorboards burst upwards or create humps like the backs of outsize camels.

Work began to replace beech wood-style laminate flooring in three rooms with a new laminate combining the ingredients of traditional laminate with linoleum and styled to resemble wood floorboards such as you might see in an old-world country pub or, nowadays, a modern bank trying to look trendy. The work took time. There was also considerable repainting of white walls and ceilings.

I'm setting the scene here.

In the midst of this, while a preppy, young university wit painter was at work, two policemen imperiously demanded to come in. I truly had no idea why they were here. As I said, I had given up hope of help to relieve my deepest agony. But over the years police officers had called unexpectedly about various issues in the building: a resident who had told the world through Facebook that he wanted to kill himself; two residents, one little and fat, one lanky and threatening, who had six times maliciously damaged the house electricity supply, cancelling lights and water (since the water pump was controlled by electricity) and thereby blocked the elevator. All such incidents had led to police calling around and sniffing out facts.

The two policemen who arrived while my flat was being repainted still had their figures in shape, one with dark hair, the other with brown and gingery locks. The two cops didn't introduce themselves or give their credentials. I didn't ask. Since they didn't tell me their names, I christened them (in my mind) as Smith and Jones, but no alias.

The dark-haired policeman began. He was Smith.

"You are Blue Sirocco?"

"Yes."

"You share the flat with Red Hawk?"

"Yes."

"Have you been arguing?"

"No," I answered. "I've been here alone all day, since about ten o'clock."

"I didn't mean just today. What about earlier in the week?"

"No," I answered truthfully for Red's verbal and physical attacks began either with some vile accusation or, if he were too drunk to be coherent, with no words at all.

"What time do you expect him back?"

"Around six."

I guessed that whatever they had come for, the cops wanted to be away before Red was back. It was as if they were fearful. Or were they protecting me from having to explain things? And to explain my plight all over again certainly would have caused me more grief.

I recovered from my general surprise and dared to challenge the copper.

"Where's all this coming from? Has somebody said anything? Who is it?"

"Yes, we've had reports but we can't say who told us."

I felt my ears burning. I thought the ears of the young painter must have been flapping merrily away.

My mind raced on, wondering who had reported my distress. I would have plumped for a caring neighbour immediately except for one thing. After his stroke, I had become Red's carer. So, I belonged to a support group, the Carers' Forum, run from a solitary building in a desert of demolition aside some defunct railway lines.

Before Covid, we used to meet once a month in any building that would allow us to meet for free. Listening to the other carers, who were mainly middle-aged or older women, I learnt that my mental and physical abuse was part of a general pattern that the other carers had all experienced although, in their cases, none of the violence had reached anything like the levels I endured from Red.

One of the Carers Forum staff who had heard some of my stories had promised her help. Was she the mysterious caller who had not only alerted the police but also said they needed to take my case seriously?

I mentioned my guess but the police responded with blank stares and no words.

Or was the informant someone who lived in our building who had heard either Red's verbal or physical assaults or both? Again, the police response was assumed incredulity.

Later the woman in social services whom I thought must have said something to the police denied having told them:

"I'm a junior here. Telling the police would be above my pay grade."

During my interview with the cops, Smith, the copper with the dark hair, went on prodding, however. It was like a police dog sniffing or a guard dog prowling, ready to pounce.

And pounce he now did.

"Does Red ever hit you?"

Well, as I've told you, that would be putting it mildly. But, since the police must surely have a record of my complaints, I wasn't going to deny it. Quite simply I answered, "Yes."

It was clear this was what the police had wanted to hear. This is what they had come for. But it was also clear that they wanted more. The sniffer policeman continued to prod. The other officer stayed silent. I sensed there was a prurient interest. And out it came.

"Are you in a relationship with Red?"

"Yes," I said.

"I knew it," said the triumphant cop.

I didn't see what that had to do with the situation. A hit, a blow, a punch was surely the same and equally criminal whatever the relationship - love, friendship, marriage or even mere acquaintance. I learned better later. But there was no time for such nicety then.

The brown-haired cop (whom I named Jones) now showed his good-cop side as he spoke for the first time.

"If this has been going on for some time why haven't you called the police?"

Call the police? I would have laughed in their faces if this hadn't been so serious. But my answer tumbled out. The little catalogue of being ridiculed; refused help from social services, my doctor and the police who had asked me to wean Red off drugs before they ever came back; the times the police had taken Red away, ferried him in their car to the outside of town, then dropped him off so that he was back as fast as his legs would take him. Listening to this, the two officers might have been abashed but, pros that they were, they hid it. Besides, they didn't want to lose the initiative.

Bad cop Smith said, "We're sorry if things could have been handled better in the past. But we are here now and from now on things will be different."

Good cop Jones said, "You have to think of your safety. These attacks may start minor but, if they're not stopped, they will get bigger, fiercer. Take action now. Accept our offer. You don't want to do nothing and end up on a mortuary slab. If Red continues on this path, he will end up killing you."

Bad cop Smith became more practical.

"Tell us how we can help you now, say with social services? If we say you need particular help, and we're the police, they won't brush you off."

So I gave them my mental shopping list of much-needed help. After all, I'd had plenty of time to think things through. You might guess what my first request was from the cops' quick response.

"We can reach social services and get them to take action like you wouldn't believe," said Smith.

It was now obvious that they wanted to be up and away before Red came back. They made it just in time.

I bore their declaration of intent in mind, waiting for them to come good. But I said nothing to Red when he came back from his session with his drinking dinosaurs.

ADVICE
Major Tip on Getting and Keeping Help

When you get the chance of a break like this muted promise of police help, no matter how unexpected and how astonishing the source, take it. Be ready as I was to tell someone in authority that, yes, you are being abused. Keep it simple. And be equally determined and precise when faced with the consequences. Remember your next chance will also come at a time of someone else's choosing. Have your script ready in your mind to slot into the next opportunity. This is what I did.

***

For a week or so things proceeded as per usual chez nous, periods of calm punctuated by drunken bouts by Red leading to petty jealousy and not so petty acts of cruelty. Then, one fine day just after lunch when Red happened to be in the flat, there came another mighty buzz on the intercom.

A voice rang out, "We're your new social workers come to see you."

Up the lift and into the flat came two contrasting types, a professional north-country lass with pure Gracie Fields social skills and a winning manner and a smart-ass Iranian-Lancashire man who was quite the polished raconteur. Her name was Gladys Knowles; his name was Reza, like the Shah who fell in the Iranian Revolution of 1979. He didn't give his last name.

So, I thought, the cops have delivered the goods, let's look at the package, then unwrap the box.

Red was surprised but thought things were looking up when Gladys said, "It was a mistake to take you off our register of vulnerable adults but we want you to know that social services will start helping you all over again."

Reza diverted Red with homespun Iranian-Lancashire tales of football and enthusiasm for Man United so that he had Red in the palm of his hand. Having softened Red up, he began asking leading questions about minor drug-taking.

I sensed lead social worker Gladys had glanced cursorily over some opera CDs on top of the sideboard. She said, "In your scenario, it sounds as if you've written the libretto yourself."

"I couldn't possibly comment," I answered.

I didn't need to guess what was happening under the surface of her mind for Gladys, now sitting demurely on the sofa, suddenly turned to me and asked sharply,

"Does Red ever hit you?"

I had been half ready for the question so my reply

was straightforward enough,

"Yes, he does."

Then I asked Gladys equally pointedly,

"The police told you to come, didn't they?"

But, like a government minister uncomfortable under a TV grilling, she would only answer indirectly,

"We're here to help. If you're ever in danger, besides calling the police on 999, contact me at this number and this e-mail address."

With that, she handed me a scruffy piece of white paper with her details scrawled on it.

The four of us said our mutual goodbyes on the pavement just outside the green front door of the building with me hoping that this Reza would give Red what he most needed: sustained social help.

In no time the police assurances earlier and the commitments of the four of us standing on the pavement that summer afternoon would be put to the test in most exacting ways.

I thought things couldn't get any more complicated. But I was wrong. They were about to. There was a spanner in the works. And it was a big one.

For years Red's money had poured through the hands of bar owners like piss streaming down a urinal, or, in his case, within a red telephone box when he couldn't hold back his wee. **After a weary Sunday night of pointless drinking,** Red was staggering down the slight hill from the Glass House bar to our home when someone he didn't know and could hardly see gave him a walloping slap. It rocked Red's head and started a cut bleeding on the side of his face. The thug grabbed Red's pudding basin hair and shoved his head down so he could bang it with his fist.

To Red, it was like his nose was going to explode. He screamed, "Oi!" then gasped for breath. He began to cough out his blood from somewhere in his throat. He was in utter terror. The crazy son of a bitch was going to kill him. It yelled,

"Give me back my five pounds, the money you stole from me in the bar!"

When Red shouted back, "I never!" his assailant punched his fist into Red's stomach, pummelling Red's torso, driving the air out of his lungs so it was all he could do to gasp. He wanted to retch but he thought he was going to choke to death.

With all his strength the guy jerked Red up and onto his feet then threw him down again. Red felt something give in his right knee as he hit the ground. The guy yanked Red up again and whirled him around, holding his arm up behind his back.

"This is what happens to petty thieves like you. Where is it, the five pounds you stole from me in the bar?"

Red shook his head. At that, the livid thief jerked Red's arm and then grunted on Red's face with his stale breath before kneeing him in the back. Red felt his right knee crumple. The guy suddenly let go of Red and when Red fell on the edge of the pavement, there was a cruel tinkling sound, so bizarre as to be almost tuneful.

∗∗∗

When my phone rang in the middle of that same night I was dazed and groggy but you-know-who's plea brought me up sharp.

"I need your help," Red croaked, slurring his words. Drunk again, but no news there. There was, however, something else. Naked fear.

"I'm round the corner by the bank that's closed down. I need five pounds."

"Five pounds? That's an odd sum."

"This man says I owe it him from just now."

"Five pounds?" I repeated. And again: "It's an odd sum. What man? What's this all about?"

"Don't ask. Please come, round the corner at the intersection. Come right away."

The phone went dead. I pressed the button on my talking clock. It was 1.05 am.

As I fumbled into my day clothes all I could think was, "Five pounds. Five pounds. How am I going to get five pounds at this time of night? The bank on the corner with the ATM has been long gone."

As I came out of the lift in my building and trailed across the squiggly corridor to the front door, and, once outside, up the gentle slope of my street that was all I was thinking about, that very precise small sum, five pounds.

When I turned into the intersection I saw them, three dark shapes next to a black cab. Up close they were Red, squatting on the pavement edge, a tall guy with tousled hair wearing a blouson-style mac, and Silent Waters, a doorman we'd known for donkey's years. Silent was a doorman at night and during the day he drove a black cab. His mum had added "Silent" to their family name "Waters" in homage to a phrase in the 23rd Psalm. Local bar staff, who thought themselves wits, used an earlier phrase in the psalm about lying down in deep pastures to call him "Deep" in awe of his long penis, whether limp or erect. They could have chosen Golden" with its double meaning for silence and balls but they had chosen "Deep."

More to the point that night Silent Waters looked as if he could land a mean punch in a split second. As an experienced doorman, he could handle all sorts of troublemakers including the tousled haired gent standing there.

God only knows how glad I was to see Silent. When I joined this sorry little group, the tousled haired guy said,

"He took five pounds from me, snatched it from me. I need it back right now."

A subtitle for this twist in the plot of Red's derangement might be, "The Mistakes of a Night," but that would imply something light and amusing, which is not what took place.

"What on earth's happened?" I asked Silent.

"I was driving past after my shift at the bar. I saw this guy bending over and thumping Red hard on the pavement. I swung my cab round. I couldn't leave Red like this."

Red was trying to sit up by raising his back and shoulders off the ground. It was also clear that Red was very, very intoxicated.

The stranger thief was a white guy with pasty coloured skin, perhaps in his late twenties. He had a podgy face and was about six feet tall. He had curly dark hair that looked like Italian hair, not tighter curled hair. [That's the tactful police phrase to prevent misunderstandings]. This stranger thief didn't want to lose control of his pathetic situation.

"I want my £10 back. I'm homeless and I need to eat."

"You just said £5."

"No. Like I told you, £12."

Silent Waters took over.

"We don't have the money. My wallet's empty. Blue's wallet's empty. Red has nothing. We're all skint."

Red, of course, was in no condition to say anything.

"I have to get home," Silent continued. "You don't want to meet my missus if I'm any later. You'd best be on your way."

To underscore his menace, Silent concluded,

"You're not getting anything from us. See the condition Red is in?"

"I need my £20," persisted the unsuccessful robber.

"Not from us, not tonight my friend," said Silent, now drawing himself up to his full height and, like a prize bull in a Picasso drawing, making the most of his powerful physique to close down any argument. Then, turning to the pitiful figure squatting on the ground, he said,

"Now, Red, get up. Let's be having you. I need to get home. I'll drop you and Blue off at yours."

"I can't stand," Red sobbed.

"Are you as drunk as that? Is that why the guy attacked you? Thought you were easy prey, easy pickings?" said Silent. "Whatever," he added. "But, like I keep saying, I need to get home to my missus and kids. Red, move yourself. Rise even if you can't shine."

The troubled robber didn't know what to say. He didn't want to leave without pickings. But he wasn't going to start a fight with three people at a major intersection that was brightly lit. He hung on, looking as wilted as an empty raincoat without a coat stand to hang onto.

Silent Waters was still on a mission.

"Red, let's have you, drunk or not."

With that, he hoisted Red, tugging him from underneath his arms and bundled him into the back of the taxi. I climbed in after him and Silent swung the taxi around the corner. When we arrived at my building, Red had no problem slumping onto the pavement and allowing Silent to drag him over to the front doorsteps, cursing all the time.

Silent did need to get home urgently. That was clear. Silent simply thought Red was just too drunk, too recalcitrant to help us help him. I was glad it wasn't me who was going to have to face Silent's formidable wife.

While we were at the doorsteps, a police car drove past on the opposite side of the street, then stopped. Two coppers got out to survey the pathetic little scene; obviously to them, it boiled down to two friends helping the third, who was helplessly drunk, into the building.

"I just can't stand," Red said piteously as he stumbled back against the steps. "Help me."

I said my heartfelt thanks and goodbye to Silent. And so began the silly business of dragging Red up the first two stone steps. Then, inside the building, Red and I faced the next four steps in the vestibule with its ornate green Victorian tiles before getting into the lobby proper with its subdued beige and brown tiles.

"Take my arm and drag me along the hall to the lift," Red gulped.

And this is what I did. Red was too far gone to curse and complain now. I got us through the first hall door into the main lobby, then along to the second door in the lobby just before the lift, into the lift and up three flights, then through the security door with its code and into the inner lobby outside the flat.

God knows the security in this building as provided by the complex system of inner doors, locks, and security codes might defeat an expert in Rubik cubes. Any malefactor might get through our front door. But, after the main lobby, he was stuck. As with Hotel California, you could check out but you couldn't leave.

I didn't appreciate these finer points that night. Believe me, pulling a drunk across a carpeted floor is more difficult than dragging him across plain laminate flooring but I managed both, more out of desperation than anything else.

However, getting this drunk, who was too heavy to lift, up into bed proved impossible. By the harsh bedroom light, I could tell that Red's jeans were badly torn at both knees. His left knee was grazed and cut. His right knee was badly swollen and pink and purple. His whole being, face, body and probably soul were dejected. He was like a creature at the end of its tether, ready to accept living death.

I gathered pillows, cushions and blankets to fashion a nest on the floor beside the bed. Red was sober enough to ask for a basin to wee in. Then he passed out.

Of course, I wanted to shout at Red that getting himself so drunk late on a Sunday night into Monday morning in a city danger spot was beyond stupid, especially if you were an alcoholic. But I didn't because, well, even on his bed on the floor, Red didn't settle.

Being scared doesn't mean that your adrenaline level kick-starts a sure-fire response. In my case that early morning it froze me into inaction. Since I couldn't see or sense how and where Red was going to hit me next, my default strategy still was to try and calm Red so we could get to the morning when daylight would let me get help for him and me.

Two or three hours later, Red started clawing at the duvet to hoist himself up and yank himself across the top of the bed and then into it. Still asleep, he kept pummelling me and began his usual tirade of personal abuse.

In the early morning, the crumpled duvet began heaving and breathing. It shifted uneasily until it assumed the body of the drunk inside it.

By 10 am Red, now sober, was in terrible trouble. Pain roared through his leg like molten lava. His body was like a death-trap of aches and pains; his right ankle was the worst, squeezing tight against his trainers, which of course we couldn't take off.

Now Red agreed I could call for an ambulance.

"Go ahead. Do it," he said with his usual grumpiness under pressure. His speech was monotonous, bitter. It was as if the wing of death had already stroked his cheek and he was getting ready for the worst life could throw at him.

We, that is to say, England was now in the brief interval between the first Covid-19 lockdown and Tier 4 restrictions and then the second full lockdown. In this late summer interlude, Covid cases were rising and, as the BBC kept telling us, the pressure was mounting on the NHS. So, I expected delays and further restrictions for Red whatever diagnosis he faced. The first hurdle would be getting an ambulance to the building.

The paramedics arrived at 1.30 pm. A slight guy and an even slighter girl, they were well up to the high standard of professional skill and generous manner we are lucky in England to have from our ambulance teams. After I gave them the short, telegram version of Red's attack, they guessed the main problem straight away. The guy told Red,

"We think a ligament at the back of your knee has been cut, either when you fell or were shoved to the ground."

Whatever Red's usual prejudice, there was no question about taking him to hospital. As I mentioned, both paramedics were slight. They couldn't carry Red to the lift. And the tight space in the flat, cluttered with heavy furniture, bookcases and odds and ends, meant that using the ambulance wheelchair was out of the question. Red had to hobble on his other leg, the one weakened by his stroke, and hold onto the furniture in the flat. Then he held onto me until we reached the lift where he could heave himself into the waiting wheelchair to take him down to, and across, the entrance hall. Finally, we came to the awkward hazard of the vestibule and its treacherous steps. There, once again, he had to shuffle on his bottom down the stone steps until clambering into the wheelchair now outside the front door.

Because of Covid's restrictions, I couldn't go with him to the hospital. I had to wait at home.

When a hospital doctor phoned half a day later, he came straight to the point,

"Red's knee is damaged in two places, at the back where his tendon was cut when he was pushed to the ground by his attacker and at the front where his knee is awry. We need to mend his ligament and realign the knee with a pin to hold it in place. The operation is tricky."

Don't think that Red was chastened by being attacked and injured. The minor hospital mishaps of life there gave him plenty of reasons for what he liked to do most: complain. There was the food,

"It's the same fucking slop every day. My own

choices on the menu count for nothing. It's always unappetising. Everyone says so. You get what you're given, not what you chose."

There were also medical delays. Having been readied for his double operation over one night and early the next day, Red's operation was postponed at almost the last minute because another patient had sudden priority since his case was more of an emergency. And the very same thing happened two days later. Red had been readied for the operation but it was postponed when the operating theatre was needed for someone else's emergency.

It may be difficult to credit but Red didn't blame the hospital.

Oh, no. He blamed me,

"It's your fault. You don't want me back. You got the operation stopped to prevent me getting out. And you don't come and see me. Three days I was in hospital before you showed your face."

This last was true. We were still in Covid-19 restrictions. When the hospital admitted Red, he had spent his first three days in semi-isolation in a reception unit while the hospital tested him and ensured he was Covid-free. As I said, I was not allowed to visit him.

By the time the operation did take place, Red was

beyond caring. When he came out of the anaesthetic his sight, his whole body felt drowsy and blurred. Red woke fitfully just in time to see the sunset beyond the window opposite his bed. Still bleary in mind and eyesight, to Red the sun was no clearer than an orange blob. He wanted the sun to fall and spill into the ward and lighten his mood. He was in for another disappointment. In his fevered mind, it looked on him no kinder than if it were an angry boil about to explode with pus.

The tricky and successful double operation on the knee and ligament did not make Red reassess his life or his behaviour. Nor did he appreciate the skilled care he received after the operation in the specialised hospital unit: palliative care, physiotherapy, exercise.

Red's always bad temper actually got worse.

If you live in a great city or a large town you can guess what our hospital looked like. From some well-intentioned Victorian buildings, red brick with white stone trim, such hospitals have developed a chain of outlying buildings connected by lumpy tentacles of concrete and brick. In Desire, the added buildings comprised an unflattering smorgasbord of 20th and 21st centuries' architectural styles. Here hospital units with such diverse specialities as Neurosurgery, Eye, ENT, Maternity, Children's, and not forgetting general hospital and A&E with its four- or five-hour waits, are yoked together on the inside by a winding passageway so long as to rival the corridor chains of the Vatican outside Rome, both thronging with people yet, somehow, deserts where no creative ideas can flourish.

During Covid restrictions, the main hospital entrances in Desire were through mighty atriums. These had glass curtain wall exteriors and, inside, cream-coloured caverns several stories high with tiny inlet doors leading to outpatient clinics and staff offices. Most visitors and staff might have been too concerned with their health problems when they arrived to take immediate artistic stock of the hospitals and their surroundings.

But patients and staff of the new Eye Hospital did take stock of their atrium. Why controversial? For, although designed as a hospital for patients with serious eye conditions, its overwhelming light from the glass roof overhead was glaring and downright uncomfortable.

After a hue and cry from the public and disabled people at the inappropriate glare in the atrium, administrators settled for wide, cream-coloured banners placed diagonally just under the glass roof on high to lessen, but not alleviate, the cruel problem of glare.

The different atriums such as Eye and Maternity opened on the outside onto a new pathway with the posh name of Sunset Boulevard. During Covid restrictions, Sunset Boulevard and the several atriums became main entrances to the hospital since the official main entrance to the north was closed. This was how I and other visitors got into the hospital and from there to the wards upstairs.

In the special unit designated for treatment and recovery of bones and limbs where Red was a patient, there still were restrictions on visiting because of Covid-19 regulations. At first, no visitors were allowed at all. Later, the ward relaxed the rules a little. If visitors could find a spare wheelchair in one of the atriums and then manoeuvre it along the long internal passageway and wind their way to the special ward, they could extricate their patient, in my case Red, for "fresh air" back along the squiggly route and again via one of the huge atriums to the pavement outside. "Fresh air" really meant an unofficial smoking area where addicts could have a fag, pollute the air, and feel guilty.

I don't really mean that very last bit.

You see, the undulating path on the outside of the calibrated, sewn-together hospitals was littered with patients and visitors hooked on tobacco. Sporadic jumbles of empty wheelchairs looked as if they were just waiting, pining, really for a trendy pop artist to collect, draw and turn them into memorials of UK popular culture, much as American artist Ben Shahn had done with trolley carts in the US.

When I fumbled along the corridors with Red in his wheelchair and then tottered along the outside pavement, his chair juddered like a worn stylus on an old LP. He would scream and curse me in exaggerated pain for my amateurishness. Out of his mouth tumbled the usual epithets: "old cunt," "blind incompetent," "fucking arsehole."

In this throwback to his persona before the attack, Red's glowering face was now the face of a sick demon.

How I dreaded my visits to the hospital and meeting any of his drinking buddies loitering outside. Red had somehow corralled them into coming by pestering them in phone calls. Once there in the unofficial smoking area, they made a conspicuous show of being Good Samaritans.

Especially odious were our visits to the ground floor cafeteria, so small and with its diminutive trail ways between tables so twisting and turning that I couldn't make a half-decent show of manoeuvring Red's wheelchair around each and every bend about tables, booths and chairs. People in the cafeteria heard and noticed Red's abuse and avoided looking at us.

As to the cafeteria food, within a day, or at most two days, you learnt to avoid meat dishes and if you really had to eat anything, to stick to the slosh of a vegetable and onion pasty and, on no account, to try anything that was supposed to be chicken (hard as any stone) or meat (inedible gristle).

Once when I was waiting for Red just outside his ward upstairs, I peered at the corridor notice board. It was full of notes and memos detailing other patients' shock and horror at the food: it was not what you had ordered; it came so late that it was cold and calcified. You name it. Any TV chef's kitchen nightmare dishes served in a dump diner would seem cordon bleu by comparison.

I wasn't the only butt of Red's rages while he was in hospital. The morning after his operation, a nurse woke Red because doctors wanted him to start moving his repaired leg. Red wasn't happy and made his fury felt across the ward,

"Get the fuck off me, you old black cow. It's still dark. I don't know what time it is. Stop touching me, fingering me up."

Another nurse joined the first to calm him.

"Red, we need to get you moving just a little to see if the operation was a success and to start you on rehabilitation and physio."

"Physio, my arse. First, you starve me to death; then when I'm still not dead like a stiff in a coffin, you yank me about like a piece of dead meat. Go get your own breakfast. Leave my leg alone."

"No, Red, that's not right. You won't get better unless you help yourself. We're here to assist. Part of your treatment is to make sure you can walk again and walk as well as possible."

Red noticed how squinty but all-seeing her eyes were as they glinted in her ample pockets of facial flesh. This stirred a terrible memory in him. Those flinty squinty eyes were almost predatory like the eyes of a Komodo dragon he had seen in a zoo or was it in a TV animal program? The eyes had a mind of their own with a prim message: "Here we are, we're coming for you. There's no escape. It won't do you any good to run. Besides, you're in no position even to contemplate that, are you?"

And, as if on cue, the pain in his knee exploded.

Eventually, the uncooperative patient allowed the nurses to stir him. But he was still not going to stir himself.

Red couldn't remember the little exercises they made

him do to get his knee moving just a little. When it was over, he wanted to drift. Whatever the slight exercises, Red was aware that his knee felt very heavy. He wondered if they had put it in a cast. He couldn't see if they had or not. They hadn't and they weren't going to. Sometimes he slept sitting propped up by pillows. He was bent like a monk in a cell, with snot trickling out of his nose.

When he stirred, he was vaguely aware of music from radios playing in neighbouring bays. He sort of saw but he couldn't be sure, patients who looked like ghouls in their hospital smocks and whom nurses trundled hither and thither in rickety wheelchairs.

This took him back to his spells in two hospitals after his stroke.

Whenever I visited him after his knee op, both of Red's knees were bandaged and some of his right leg also. But, after he began to recover a little from his exercises and physio, he took a photo of the more damaged leg without its bandages. The scar of the operation ran from above the front of his knee way down his leg. It was long and wide, a deeply disturbing cavern excavated by the knife. It was, to put it politely, dramatic and unsettling, though Red told me the scar would close in time. Even so, the pitiful sight was not for the squeamish, and that included me.

You won't be surprised to know it was a relief, after my visits, to walk home by myself away from the hospital and Red's rages. And it often came during my favourite time of day when late afternoon was preparing for night. Slate-coloured roads turned to evening cerulean; street lights shimmered like yellow sparklers; and homeward bound traffic whirred up dust when it was dry, or danced and splashed across puddles when it was wet, like a squirting shower. The yellow street lights turned everything ever darker blue. In my individual sight, everything blurred the sight of buildings and pedestrians as night descended like a parachute to envelop the city. I used to love it. And I breathed a sigh of relief, but it was temporary.

Of course, I wasn't free from Red. So determined was he to get out of hospital that he galvanised himself through exercises and physio, cursing staff all the while, but working through the pain to achieve some limited mobility with a view to escape.

In response to Red's utmost desire, after a few more days, an indecent interval, the hospital tried to ready him and me for his return to the flat. I quailed. I dreaded caring for someone who needed so much looking after and was always ready to dish out physical violence in return.

The doctors told Red at his bedside and me on the phone that, when he first came out of hospital, he would have to use a wheelchair. As a disabled person myself I knew the politically correct phrases. You never spoke about people being "confined to a wheelchair" but, instead, described them as "wheelchair users."

Correct vocabulary was not my problem, however. It was the size of my small flat and the important furniture within it. You might say it was cluttered; I might admit it was overcrowded. Either way, anyone using a wheelchair would have mammoth problems in my building. First were the high steps at either entrance, too high to make a slope with wood because you couldn't get up it and, going out, you would whoosh and tumble down. Then there were the complex series of security doors on each floor. And I didn't see how Red and I would manage easily once Red was confined to my floor; nor could I see how I could manage him, his temper, and my safety.

Of course, any NHS hospital is always under pressure to move existing patients and release their beds for new patients. This was especially true during the first major Covid crisis.

However, Red's imminent release came with a warning.

One of the doctors phoned me as Red's official carer and laid it out,

"Once Red recovers sufficiently in hospital and can be discharged, he has to follow medical instructions to the letter. If he falls or doesn't take care and damages the knee again, it may be possible to operate a second time on his damaged ligament but success is more problematic. The damage to his knee so far and the cuts in the first operation left less flesh and sinew and muscle for a surgeon to work with. And if there is another fall or more damage, there's no chance of a third operation; he would be on crutches after that or need to use a wheelchair permanently."

This warning heightened my apprehension. Again, I tried stalling Red's release. That worked just briefly because his progress through physiotherapy and rehabilitation exercises was so impressive, apparently, that his doctors dropped the idea of a wheelchair and decided he could, instead, walk with a Zimmer frame to begin with and a metal cane or crutch later on.

I tried stalling again. Bill Strethers, the liaison man at the hospital, agreed to come to my flat. He said on the phone,

"Call me Bill. I can see if the flat is suitable and, if not, what might be done within it to make it so.

"Do you mind if I come early tomorrow?" Bill asked. "Coming at 7.30 am. If there's a problem, I'll be sure to call you and then come at 8.30 am."

I agreed. The next day 7.30 am came and went. No Bill. Then 8.30 am came and went without phone call or explanation from Call me Bill.

When I called the hospital, liaison man Bill wasn't available but I could leave a message. Successive half hours came and went without the inspection of the apartment or any explanation. After 4.30 pm the man did call but not to apologise. Oh, no. Please don't think he ever would.

"I missed you," Bill began unapologetically. "I'd forgotten I was doing the school run for my kids today," he added with a giggle as camp as any geisha playing with her fan.

Well, the joke was on me for believing I would get advice, if not help, from Call me Bill, someone who didn't give a fig.

Real insult followed. What I didn't know until later was that getting ready to discharge Red, hospital psychiatrists had examined Red that same day to see if he was well psychologically. Apparently, he passed the test with flying colours. Considering that hospital staff on the ward could not but be well aware of Red's temper tantrums, this was astonishing.

Was it that the examiners were not good at their job? That they asked the wrong questions? Or that their tests were not appropriate? Either way, it was not the hospital that bore the brunt of their inexcusable mistake. It was helpless me. I thought that the examiners who passed Red as fit for human consumption in the home should have had to consider their position. Any chance of that? You know the answer.

To repeat, the brunt of Red's escape from hospital was borne by yours truly. Here's what happened.

The hospital ambulance crew who ferried Red home were nothing like the skilled and courteous paramedics who had taken him to hospital two weeks previously. These were surly, discontented taxi drivers only too eager to drop Red and me off outside the building and, heeding his order to vamoose, drivers who then failed to ensure he got safely into the flat. Simply unprofessional.

After his release, Red's hospital check-up three weeks later had an adverse effect on his behaviour. It was like releasing a cork out of a liquor bottle.

Red no longer needed the Zimmer frame. He could now walk with a metal crutch. And it was not long before he could manage more timidly unaided. That was good.

Then we went back to the hospital for them to look over Red and his knee. After an hour waiting for his check-up in the hospital, a nurse announced to patients and their supporters,

"We're sorry. Due to a mistake in communication, the surgeon cannot be with us this afternoon. He's been double booked and is in an operating theatre in another hospital north of here. However, our other doctors will attend to everyone who agrees to stay."

Red, who had been chafing at the bit because of the delay, did agree to inspection by a junior doctor. Then came two different verdicts and prescriptions. A senior charge nurse told me,

"Red has to stay at home with plenty of bed rest and move only with the Zimmer frame."

However, when the junior doctor had surveyed Red, it was a different story,

"Red can move freely unaided; he needn't return to hospital unless something goes wrong. We've removed the dressing on his leg where he had cuts and abrasions. We've just changed his dressings on the other leg where he had the knee surgery. We'll arrange for district nurses to come to the flat and change his dressings two or three times a week."

I had dreaded such news, so cavalier a medical

opinion. And with it, I knew, as I said, the cork would explode from the bottle of Red's pent-up alcoholism and alcohol-driven fury. And this was going to happen as sure as eggs are eggs. And it did.

Within a few days, two district nurses came to change Red's dressings. Strong, capable and authoritative, the lead nurse explained the process to the junior nurse and also to Red, the do's and don'ts of his still precarious medical condition.

When they finished, I went with them downstairs to the front door of the building. My own pent-up frustration at the awkward situation the hospital had put me in and my fear of Red's reprisals simply cascaded out.

"Before Red's attack and injury on the street, the police came to me, explaining that Red's explosive temper and his attacks on me, which other people had told them about, were putting me in extreme danger. The hospital ignored my concerns. My sense of duty is strong but, given Red's record, it feels as awkward and painful as new shoes that don't fit. I know I cannot give Red the care he needs as he recovers from his injury and the surgery. And I'm afraid of what he will do."

The lead nurse's answer astonished me. I had been so used to people in authority brushing away my fears that

I was not ready for her candid, supportive advice.

"You must do what is right and best for you, not him. If you need protection from the police or counselling from social services, don't hesitate to ask for it. Don't wait until it's too late."

I was heartened by support from an unexpected quarter. Had the nurse peered below the surface and detected a simmering threat from Red, or was she simply an experienced practitioner who knew that carers had rights just as much as the people they looked after?

I needed her counsel more than ever over the next bitter few days.

The following afternoon Red was off to the Glass House and when he returned drunk as a skunk it was as if his accumulated fury from the past weeks was erupting like a volcano. I had expected hurt and anger from him to burst like an exploding pressure cooker but not this no-holds-barred fury.

"You're in for it now, you timorous little beastie. I'm gonna pay you back for all the lying and cheating you've done since I went into hospital and after. Don't try and deny it. As I look at you, you worn-out old tramp, it's so clear what one of your damned writers says, 'Age is no guarantee of respectability.' That might have been specially written about you, quivering with shame. It probably was. You're old enough."

Then it came, whack across my face with his phone.

"Don't be surprised," he said agreeably. "You should have seen it coming."

My heart was beating fast, far too fast. It wasn't only that Red had startled me. Had he also seen into my mind and detected a secret plan against him that he had not even thought possible until that very moment? Red saw something was wrong. It would not have occurred to him that it was him; it must be with me.

Nevertheless, I did say lamely,

"It's not you; it's me."

"You don't know what it is, do you, judgy? You who judges everyone else?" he replied to his own question.

Red's voice was harsh, scolding, just as I imagined his grandmother's voice must have been when she was angry with one of her kids and grand kids, not, of course, ever angry with him, her favourite grandchild.

Despite my own paralysing fear, I sensed his whole body was juddering even as he cracked his bitter vocal whip.

"Well, judgy, there's a lot wrong with your life, what with all your affairs on the side, your guilt eating you from the inside out."

I hadn't been having sex on the side. It was one of

Red's insecure fantasies, one that he had troubled dreams about. He calmed himself down and switched on the TV as if nothing was wrong.

That night when Red thrashed about the bed moaning, I did wake up. This was a new pattern of behaviour. He would talk as if someone else was in the room. He would answer himself with their inarticulate replies, inarticulate to me, that is. When he woke and I dared to ask him about these troubled dreams, Red always said he couldn't remember anything.

Red's behaviour now went rapidly downhill. There were days of abject drunkenness and one when he became furious at my serving him a Marks and Spencer's steak and ale pie with a vegetarian Kiev that he denounced as "Paki food."

Red hurled the Kiev at me, my clothes and body. He repeatedly threw three TV remotes at my head and shoulders. When they came apart, he made furious demands that I reassemble them. Then he repeated the throwing and his demands for repair. Lastly, he lobbed fruit at me and around the flat.

I was terrified that evening and through much of the night. And frightened also on the following afternoon and night when Red was livid that I wasn't back in the flat at 2 pm as he had expected.

While I was out, in his drunken anger at my delay Red had turned over my papers and scattered them, emptied one drawer and turned it upside down to let loose the contents. Out of the middle drawer of the little chest he had already damaged, the sleeve of an old pullover stuck out like a naughty tongue.

When I got back, Red was looking over a spare sheet of paper on my desk with a list. It read: "Bitter sweet, living dead, skinny broad, true lies, idiot savant, wise fool, clumsy grace."

"What's this?" he barked. "It's rubbish. It makes no sense. You're meant to be writing. This is just gibberish. You can't publish this."

"It's a list of oxymorons," I answered. "They're combinations of words that set two opposites together that do have a joint meaning. Like *idiot savant*, that's a person with learning difficulties but who does have some outsize gift or acquired wisdom. I'm making a list to see if I can use them all in one sentence."

"Well, that's not going to happen. You're talking nonsense, just like you always do. But you can't kid me. I'll give you oxy-whatever."

With that, he tore the paper.

"Ripped in two, just like you said, blockhead."

And that trivial trigger egged him on in the round of

mayhem he had already started. Red saw my dismay at the mess of papers and odds and ends. He grinned. As if taking a high moral ground he said like a dismissive old professor,

"You look on the manuscripts of your books like A levels to be marked by a hostile examiner. But no one's interested. No one's gonna read your books. Not now. Not with this mess. Writer of the century? Give me a break."

Apprehension spread across my face like deathly pallor. But underneath Red's drunken bravado I knew he, too, was afraid because, no matter how frightened I looked, there was a part of me he could not touch: the writer, whether good, bad or indifferent, the writer he had insulted. He wanted to see fear. He wanted to control me. Part of his sporadic assaults was psychological, more mental cruelty than physical attack or damage to property.

There was plenty of implied physical assault, however. He wanted to rev the fear of God in me that evening by hitting me again and again, each time closer to my face, knowing that battering my face might tip what little eyesight I had into defenceless blackness.

And so that evening Red moved toward me with surprising sure-footedness considering how drunk he was, raising his arm with a TV remote control over his shoulder and swinging it as if he was about to bowl out a test cricketer from India or Pakistan.

The remote whooshed as he spun it through the air, missing the outsize wall mirror but landing on my neck with a mighty thwack. The remote snapped open, sending its batteries who knows where across the room. Red bared his teeth.

"I wanna see shame in your face and terror in your eyes before you admit you deserve every bruise and thwack."

He folded the day's Metro paper and slapped my face with it. Then he hit my side and my ass as I tried to move away. I wasn't going to fight back. That would only have spurred him on and, of course, he was far more experienced, far better at this, than I was. One of his favourite sayings was, "I love a good scrap."

Was this a loveable scrap when the odds were so unfair? A weary old man versus a drunken brute?

"Don't you ever try and get away from me. Pick it up," Red barked, meaning the broken remote. "Put it back together. I'm speaking to you, dozy head. Pick the remote up, get the batteries wherever they are, under a chair, at the edge of the carpet. Do it and do it right now."

With that, he forced me onto my knees and bashed my shoulders with the paper. It was senseless pummelling. It got worse as I stumbled on my knees to locate the batteries which I couldn't see. He reminded me who was the boss by more thwacks.

Later, his arm ached and he took codeine pills to ease the pain.

Don't think I was sorry for him.

When he was drunk like this, he was most angry for what he might have missed while he was in a pub. What had I been doing? With whom? How often? Each of his imagined scenarios spelt one thing to him, I was defying him. He liked to think I had asked for his violence, actually invited it.

That twilight evening, he drove me along the floor, raining blows with the Metro paper and sometimes kicking me while I tried to cradle my head from his blows. The only sounds were my breathing, my hesitant gasps.

This large living room had a handsome sideboard, a Victorian imitation of Queen Anne style and an accompanying breakfast table and chairs with suitably bowed legs. There was also a 1920s cocktail cabinet, implausibly in the same imitation Queen Anne style. All were self-proclaimed mahogany like the slab top of the sideboard but most were rosewood coloured darker red-brown to look like mahogany.

Earlier in the day, I had sorted out various small glass bottles and plastic containers on this mahogany sideboard top. Red used the bottles as yet more missiles, throwing them at me, one or two at a time. Some broke on the laminate floor. When he picked them up he got an unpleasant surprise when one cut his fingers. One cut was like scratches, others were nasty gashes.

When he bent down to curse me as I was grovelling on the floor, a spare jar of lanolin perched on the sideboard hit him square on his left eyebrow. He struggled to see through the goo already smeared on the jar top. Through his blurred vision, he realised that I may have been a cowering figure but he suspected that the fear spreading across my face was not fear of him but fear of something else. What exactly? He couldn't be sure.

I knew. It was fear of what I had to do, the steps I had to take whatever the obstacles of scorn and delay by official bodies along the way.

I began by daring Red, saying,

"I'm not afraid of you, you little fat fuck."

This wasn't true. I wanted my rebuke to come out like a clarion denunciation but what came out of my mouth sounded more like a timid little tootle. For far too long I had lain in bed every night wondering what form his reign of terror would take next.

To repeat myself, this was downtown in a city centre. We were not living in an ultra-nice bourgeois home with neatly manicured front gardens and pristine windows with lavish curtains that hid all sorts of indiscretions. Here we lived cheek by jowl in an apartment building converted from a warehouse. We were so near the organisations that could help us, such as the police and social services but also so far away, given their refusal over the years to pay anything more than lip service to help and mostly not even that.

What I wanted above all was the exhilaration of ordinary life, the huzz and buzz of street life, to be able to stop and stare beyond the moon at the stars, although I knew that was not possible with my warped sight, not this all-pervasive claustrophobia hurtling to some inevitable crash ending.

That fateful evening, Red's choice was scattergun theatrics, pitiful, puny efforts with tiny missiles, but cutting nevertheless both in living room and hall. After I got to my feet still trembling, I grasped the gold occasional table in the bedroom where I had also tried to put small containers in order. But I upset the table.

To defend myself, I pushed it towards Red as it fell. It pirouetted on one leg like a ballet dancer in *Nutcracker*. The mirror hanging on the wall just above the table came off its moorings and shimmied, squinting its reflection across the room like a helter-skelter effect in a Hollywood cartoon. Glass seemed to fly like a hail of arrows.

The sharp edge of the table's loaded glass top bit into Red's side and tipped him off balance. And so, this top, laden with bottles of pills and canisters of deodorants, belched its contents across the floor; cough medicines spilt out like dirty spittle among yet another of Red's festival of glass shards. A stray nail on the floor nipped Red's feet. It squealed like some nasty little rodent that didn't like being stepped on one little bit. Red cursed it.

As I looked towards Red, it was difficult amid the horrible shambles of bedroom and hall to recall that I had once loved this terrifying, drunken, emotionally deformed Caliban creature, now quivering with rage and hurt before me. Yet I had. But that did not mean that I wasn't still afraid of him nor that, at this moment and others, I didn't wish him dead. Worse, I hated myself, no matter how lonely I had once been, for ever allowing him into my life. While he still shivered in his drunken stupor, I was mortally afraid that my terrifying experience would take first my sanity and then my life.

I moved cautiously across the broken glass to get a brush and pan from the kitchen. Red was raging.

"If you call the police - go on, do it - I'll beat the shit out of them. They won't take me easily; remember that time I stood my ground and fought them in the pub? They're like cattle, old and fat just like you."

I was surprised Red could say so much and so coherently because he was also hurt by his own actions. His eyes seemed to swell and his fingers seeped blood over his hands.

Delicately he picked up a shard of glass, tawdry remnant of a broken chandelier. While I was still quivering, he bent over me, holding the glass at my cheek. First he grazed my skin. Then with a little dent he cut it slightly so that the blood gulped into a diminutive trickle and then settled into a sticky blob.

"Let's see what they have to say when they see how you broke my mouth," he added, much to my surprise. With that, he spat out part of a tooth.

I would have preferred him to choke on it.

With a furious cry, he charged on to me, banging his fists on my chest. His expression was outraged, perplexed and terrible to look at. There was no more dashing Red now. My old friend and partner had gone. I felt deep sorrow, darker than the fear of being hit. As I looked at this strange creature with this grimy, insulting leer on its face, I felt paralysed by a stinking fear, stinking because it felt wet as if someone had pissed all over me and I couldn't dry myself. This imagined stink came from my nagging uncertainty, that it was all my fault.

"How well you arranged things, Red," I thought when I was in the other room. For someone who wasn't in the least intellectual, it was as if he was as good as any top-flight chess player. "Yes, Red," I thought again, "no matter how perplexed, you're manipulating me, pulling my strings and making me wobble, cringe, and collapse. You might feel some pity for me and what you're doing. But no. So, this is how you take your revenge on all the people you blame for mistreating you. Bully me, the one person who has been truly kind to you over the years. It's creepy. It's worse than creepy, it's evil."

He bawled my name twice, "Blue Belle, Blue Belle," adding, "Get your pinched arse in here! Now!" Then pausing for a moment, he reflected, saying, "You don't know the first thing about me."

Been with the guy for almost twenty years and I didn't know anything about him? I wondered if many of us abused wives, husbands and partners who found out too late what our abusers were like inside would agree with me. And how many of us have known for some time but have been trapped with no realistic prospect of escape?

For years I had been cowed by his furious rages. Sometimes I had held back from reporting molestation out of fear of what he would do. And, as I've said, in the past so many organisations supposed to help had turned me down.

Now I felt different. The double whammy of two nights' assaults back-to-back galvanised me to retaliate. It was now or never. I had to complain, seek police help no matter what the risk and stare down police contempt. By now I had an ally, Jack Rascal.

ADVICE
Escape Routes

What is the problem? Domestic abuse. What's my solution?

What I've tried in this book is to show you, to explain, what and how I have learnt from my successes and my mistakes. We're not going to resolve the problems of the police, social services and the courts or to make their office politics and internal squabbles go away. No, but we have to utilise them.

My interest is you, my reader.

Nothing is more important than your survival. Domestic abuse threatens survival. Since a core part of our brains is the instinct to survive what I write is relevant to you. And there can hardly be a more important subject than survival from domestic abuse in the years of Covid-19.

But there are significant roadblocks en route to freedom. If you're getting beaten up, will courts protect you?

TAKE ACTION

The original idea underlying my novel was to dramatize the abuse I suffered and by referring to it to spur any of you who've suffered domestic abuse on to constructive action. I would like you to reassess your situation realistically to take effective action. Or to take action to help your dear ones who have suffered.

So, if you can't get to courts to protect you, which routes might you take?

6 Tips for Action

1. Take from my story what seems most relevant to you. Tackle domestic abuse through the agencies that are supposed to help, even though, initially, as I said, two of them turned me down: police and social services - and there are also the unreliable courts. In other words, deal with the problem on several fronts. What you need on your route to safety are persistence and stamina.

2. And among the most crucial things you can do if you are a victim of abuse, or you are the friend or family member helping the victim, is to be ready with a quick-fire, seemingly spontaneous request for help if, by chance or design, you unexpectedly catch someone who can help you.

   This could be a sympathetic police officer, a kindly councillor or a committed social worker. You may come upon them in an elevator, crossing a car park, in the lobby of an official building, or a supermarket, a newsroom or library and even a doctor's practice. And you may only have moments to get their attention, spark their interest, and press your case for action.

3. What is essential to do this is to have a carefully prepared, seemingly unprepared and superficially

spontaneous little speech in plain, precise English at the ready to get your potential new friend onside. As you plan your short sentences, visualise the person you want to reach. Get your message in the right order.

In these maybe once-in-a-lifetime opportunities, you have to be single-minded, ruthlessly so, if you like. Be concise. Cut out qualifications. You can include complications or nuances later as necessary.

Let's give ourselves a time limit. You've got three minutes. Go! Now!

4 Don't rest content if your target audience tries to fob you off by directing you to a website. This website response is typical of some politicians and it resounds badly on them if people sense evasion.

Your aim is stark: How to get out of an abusive relationship yourself, or to help a friend or family member to do so.

5 How to get the police, social services or the courts to help you.

If you start a process, of persuading the police, arguing your case in court, or convincing social services that it is their duty to intervene and help you, you will face opposition.

So, in your mind's eye, get ready to answer any

potential hostile questions to see if you are ready to wow them into silence and submission.

6. Here are points to consider. The following section is inspired by chapter six of leading copywriter Steve Harrison's *How to Write Better Copy* (2016). His well-honed truths have universal application way beyond commercial advertising.

I don't say the following to be hostile but rather so that you are ready with a put-down phrase to get around, to deflect, any deliberate obstacles to understanding. Here are two abrupt questions that will take away your target audience's breath and draw them up sharp:

Are they scared that your abuser knows more than you or they do?

Are you or they worried that a court will reject your claim?

Once it comes to these and any other reservations or qualifications by your target audience, say you understand why anyone might be hesitant and have doubts. In short, factor in your audience's possible resistance. Disarm them by saying something like, "I realise you don't know me; you haven't even heard of me. You may be wondering if you can trust me, since we've never been introduced formally. But you can trust me. And I need you."

Here are 3 lead questions that use a technique of the surprise we call abruption:

1 Do your potential allies have two hours to kill in Desire? Meaning will they resist helping you, knowing full well that if they won't do something positive and supportive, this could lead to your death tonight?
2 And if they won't help you, then why ever not? Find a way of putting the onus, the responsibility, onto them.
3 Do they want their home town to be known as the UK capital of domestic abuse? [This is a daring abruption].

Just as readers get engaged when they can see themselves in a novel, short story, or crime report, remember that your unexpected target audience needs to see themselves stuck in the problem you are explaining to them and want to escape from.

After you explain your problem, draw your target in further with a superficially inclusive question such as, "Hasn't anything like this happened to you or anyone in your family in your own home? Well, it has certainly happened to me."

What you are trying to do is to win your once-in-a-lifetime audience over by playing upon their presumed natural human sympathy, even if this sympathy is far from immediately obvious.

Once you have piqued your audience's interest, then swivel the story around to include them, to turn their interest into a desire to help you. Here play on their undoubted store of common humanity and decency.

If they have some official job that shouldn't be difficult. They cannot in all honesty deny your just request for help. If they do, ask how they spell their name and to name the specific organisation they work for. That is the precise department in a precise council, the precise name of a police force or the name of their NHS trust.

If you try all or some of this and they still deny you, then their failure gives you a pressing reason you need to approach their organisation. Oblige the organisation to help where their malfunctioning employee would not.

EPISODE 5

For Whom The Bell Tolls

Just when you least expect it, you may get help and help from an unexpected quarter. As I hinted, this was exactly what did happen to me.

I was coming home with two heavy shopping bags, cursing the massive scaffolding for mighty repair around a nearby building. Why? To convenience the owners and inconvenience everyone else, the council had closed the bus stop in front of the scaffolding for two years.

From behind me, a voice said, "Hi!"

I turned. There stood a once-muscular guy in blue jeans, bulging T-shirt and black baseball cap. He was now out of shape. I didn't recognise him. And yet there was something familiar, something also heavy and sinister about him. But he was friendly at the same time.

"You don't remember me, do you? Well, it's been a while. It's Jack, Jack Rascal. You must remember when I hoisted Red back onto his feet when he fell backwards down the steps of Tricks. He was at someone's birthday bash."

"Of course," I answered as if by rote because, although I remembered the incident, it had been dark and I couldn't equate this man out to cadge my friendship with any of Red's birthday revellers.

"I've changed, haven't I?" he continued.

I didn't say anything. He repeated his name. I had

never known it.

"It's Jack, Jack Rascal. I was working on the door the night Red fell. I was sorry to hear he had a stroke shortly afterwards."

"That's right," I murmured but I was playing for time until my memory kicked in and I could better identify this Jack Rascal.

Then, instead of some pleasantry about how he hoped Red had recovered, Jack shifted the conversation to himself.

"I don't work on the doors any longer. That's probably why you haven't seen me around. One night I was attacked outside the pub by a group of rowdies with a grudge; beaten up badly. I was in hospital for two weeks recovering."

I was lost for words. But Jack Rascal shifted gear again.

"You live near here, don't you? You're struggling with your bags. Let me take them and you to your front door."

"I appreciate the gesture. But I think it might cause problems."

"Red trouble, eh? Jealous as ever?" he said, clearly disappointed.

"But we can go to the coffee shop nearby," I

suggested. It's just across the street from where I live."

"My flat, too. I'd appreciate that."

And so, with Jack Rascal carrying half the shopping, that's what we did. I signed us in with the (then) obligatory Covid restriction order. Jack had a cappuccino and I had an American. We were served by a young Australian guy with black hair, tattoos peeping out of his short sleeves and open shirt, all of which Jack clearly admired. That amused me and helped lighten a heavy conversation.

When two people meet and the meeting can be casual or intense, and whatever the relationship between them is going to be, there comes a moment, specific to these individuals when they exchange a password, spoken or by gesture, that each of them likes the other. Often that moment is so casual, so insignificant seeming that it can pass the two people by without them remembering it. Translated into words, it is no more than, "I like you."

Something of the sort happened during our inconsequential meeting over coffee when Jack Rascal was not drooling over his Australian cutie, for we both genuinely did like one another. We didn't savour the moment at the time because Jack was consumed with his fall from good health and physical grace after his being beaten outside the pub where he had worked as a doorman.

My personal problems seemed small beer by comparison but they provoked a big reaction in Jack. He noticed a bruise on my cheek below my right eye and a cut on the other side.

"You've never complained. But I can surmise what's going on with you and Red. You haven't fallen over a chair or bumped into a door. He's been hitting you."

That was enough to burst the dam of silence that had kept my fears and my emotions locked up from the outside world. I told him what you, dear readers, know, my story so far. Jack didn't respond with sympathy but with instructions.

"You have to bring matters to a head. You cannot let things drift with you getting hurt every time Red feels like it. I'm sorry to say it, but I think you're in denial about how serious your situation is."

But then with Jack, it was back to his own problems of denial. With problems at work in his new job of housing maintenance and no longer having a partner to share the rent, Jack simply didn't have enough to live on.

"I don't like to ask but can you help me out with money for food and my dog. She's a border collie, as well as a life saver."

"Here's £20."

It was all the spare money I had.

My experience of life so far had taught me that when people help you, rarely is it for nothing. As Americans used to say about their bars, "There's no free lunch." And once anyone sees you as a sympathetic ear, an easy touch, this can become a very dangerous steep slope.

But for the present Jack urged me to do what I had tried and failed to do before - go back to the police and ask for some form of protection.

"I'll come with you," he said. "No backsliding."

So, this Jack Rascal was going to come with me to the police station opposite the Town Hall. And he was determined to hold firm whether I lost my nerve or not. We set a day - Monday - when we would go to the police together and he would back me up.

"The police might ignore one lonely supplicant," he said. "They won't do so if there's a second person there as a witness."

When the fateful Monday arrived, I faced such a battery of phone calls about bank and mortgage business that I did lose my nerve and decided to postpone. Jack was having none of it. He sent me a terse, withering e-mail,

"You can't do this to yourself, postpone and

postpone. You have to follow through on your resolve, especially since Red's attacks and your injuries are so fresh. Some things you just have to do, even if there is a risk that everything doesn't go according to plan. That's the first important thing I learned when I was a teenager. And," he added grimly, "I didn't find it out from my parents. If you don't act, you'll spend the rest of your life in misery."

I answered, "OK, you win. We'll do it your way. Let's try again tomorrow, Tuesday. I'll wait for you outside your building at 10 am."

And so, on Tuesday I called at his apartment building which was near mine, sat on the lengthy front steps fit for a Joan Crawford entrance in a 1930's Hollywood movie until he arrived. Then we trod our weary way to the police station and went in.

When I rang the bell for attention, in my feverish mind it rang around the reception room like an ominous sound effect in a symphony, not summoning everyone to attention but sounding a death knell for the whole human race.

"I need your help and protection. I'm a victim of sustained domestic violence."

That's how I began to the shadowy figure on the other side of the reception window. You can tell I had rehearsed my words beforehand. Otherwise, I would have stuttered into incompetence.

"Wait by the seats opposite and we'll get someone to interview you," said the Voice.

Note that the Voice didn't tell us to *sit* on the seats opposite. They were cordoned off with yellow tape to forestall Covid infection by proximity.

In no time we were ushered into an interview room where a policewoman and policeman were ready for us. She had a charming manner and he was in awe of her. She explained that they were both based at another police station and on loan as guest artists for the day.

I began my tale of woe: how I had been with Red for eighteen years or so, how, ever since he had been made homeless a second time he had started living with me officially and was registered on the electoral roll, etc.; how from dim beginnings his violence to me and our shared flat had spiralled out of control with broken ornaments and furniture, my slashed hand, Red's continuous threats, etc.

Jack not only backed me up but also elaborated on points that he thought essential to prove his credentials as a true-blue friend and how perilous were my physical situation and psychological state.

The policewoman ran through a list of options open

to me, carefully stressing that they could not give direct advice, and making photocopies of documents detailing possible courses of action. By the way she spoke, it was clear that her preferred option was a domestic violence protection order that the police could begin to process and impose.

2 Escape Routes for Victims of Domestic Violence
Here are some escape routes and official explanations about them:

1 Domestic Violence Protection Notices (DVPNs) are frequently issued by police when attending incidents of alleged domestic violence.

 The purpose of a DVPN is to get the troublemaker out of the property for 48 hours. The police follow temporary removal with an application to a magistrate's court for a DVPO to remove the offender from the premises for a further 28 days.

 The thinking behind the order is to give the victim of domestic violence a breathing space in which to seek help and assistance and consider their options.

2 A Domestic Violence Protection Order (DVPO) is an order made by a magistrates' court after a DVPN has been issued. A DVPO may be in force for between 14 and 28 days, beginning on the date it is

made by the magistrates' court.

Background to these measures

The Domestic Violence Act 1995 made psychological abuse an offence. It provides victims with means of protection. It defines psychological abuse as "including intimidation, harassment, damage to property, threats of physical, sexual or psychological abuse, and (in relation to a child), abuse causing or allowing the child to witness the physical, sexual or psychological abuse of a person with whom the child has a domestic relationship".

***

Acknowledging these two routes, Jack said, "Blue is in danger of Red's violence. He needs help now."

"We can provide that," said the charming policewoman. "We've set a marker on your phone number. If you call the police because Red still tries to get back into the flat, the police will come straight away."

To Jack's consternation, not to say irritation, once again I demurred about which course of action to take as regards any police action but I promised to think things through and return the next day with a clear decision.

"You missed a rare opportunity," Jack said after we left the interview. "They would have acted immediately. But you still have a golden opportunity to rid yourself of the troll once and for all. Don't delay again."

The fact that the police had been so cordial and I now had a route to escape more domestic abuse filled me with more confidence than I had felt for years.

Guiding Principal When You Go to a Police Station
What I learned most from my visit to the police with Jack alongside was, if you are making a complaint to the police, if at all possible, go with a good friend or a sympathetic family member. If there are two of you, the police are more likely to be professionally aware and on their guard since they know a third party is listening to how they handle your complaint. So, you have a witness to the police conversation.

But I am not pretending that this is a guarantee of police action and cooperation.

***

You see, the next day Jack and I went back to the police station by the Town Hall and the result was very different.

I rang the designated bell for attention somewhat

timidly. It was as if I had no right to be there. Again, I looked around the lobby of the police station carved into a corner of a council building. I didn't have long to wait. An old cop appeared with rumpled shirt and rumpled hair, what there was of it. He was polite, uninterested and determined not to be bothered.

With a heavy heart, he swung his outsize eye-popping tummy into the small glass-fronted cubicle cut into the long reception desk. He listened patiently enough to my recap about my interview with the kind officers the previous day. He answered as if by rote, "I can't get involved in this. We need to get you the officers who interviewed you yesterday. They're at another police station. If I get involved, it could mess things up for you. I'll get a message to their station."

"I'm ready to go there," I suggested.

"No. Wait here."

And that was what we had to do.

I sensed that the old cop was feeling the same sort of things I was feeling myself. You could tell by his thoughtful expression, not like a copper in his sixties but with the fearful eyes of the child he had been fifty years earlier. I was thinking, "I'm scared." And I guessed he was thinking he was scared as well, scared of having to get up off his lazy fat ass and do something about a tricky situation. I realized that I was interpreting him not as a policeman but as a frail and faulty human being just like me.

I was unnerved by police rejection of my plan of escape from Red and his persistent abuse, sure enough. But I wasn't done. I still clung to the promise of the previous day's nicer Punch and Judy police officers that I should get Red turned away by the police if he tried to get back into the flat.

If only it had been so simple.

As I said before, there were few seats in the police lobby. Most of them had strips of yellow tape as a sign that Covid restrictions forbade us to sit. I sat on the wide ledge of a window facing the side entrance to the old Town Hall itself, a Victorian building designed with several facades like backdrops for a German romantic opera. Jack sat on one of the few available metal chairs.

We waited and waited so long there that our minds got as numb as our butts. People with other problems came into the police station, rang the bell, and were told to wait. But the comings and goings did not relieve our deadening monotony. From time to time, one of us would go to reception, ask politely what, if anything, was happening to our case. Each time we were given the same stock answer:

"Everything is in hand; we've e-mailed the other police station."

Jack was anxious about a doctor's appointment. I felt acutely for him because he was my only friend. So, I was more frustrated for him than for myself. I suggested we tell the officers we had to leave for his sake but would come back in the early afternoon.

Walking home, Jack chided me,

"You see this is what happens because you didn't get the police to set their own restrictive order against Red yesterday when they were ready to do it there and then."

After Jack's doctor's appointment, we returned to the police station, our hopes somewhat muted. And it was the same procedure, the same story, all over again; the police would not get involved in a problem first recorded the previous day. We were told quite sharply to sit and wait for a response from officers in the other station.

The weary wait through the afternoon was like a parody of ground hog day with no end in sight amid the dour cream walls, the outsize shop-style windows. Everything was devoid of personality in a waiting room miraculously worn down by countless footfalls and yet, at the same time, a strange ghost room. It was as if we had never been there at all. As darkness began to settle,

I knew I had to get home sharp since, whenever darkness descended, my eyesight would retreat until the next day. When that happened, I could hardly see outdoors.

Jack walked me home. He said dejectedly, "I can't believe that, after prolonged separate morning and afternoon sessions in the police station, not a single officer would help us." Then he added, "Do you have £10 so I can get milk and bread and dog food?"

Once I was home, Jack returned to the police station by himself to remonstrate with a different set of police officers who had started on a later shift.

On the outside he projected a sense of kindly authority I associated with a good dad, not that I had a good dad. Mine was absent, if you get my drift. But now Jack was trying to take such effortless charge of my problems, I was in danger of self-deceiving hero worship. I lived with the promise of escape from Red in my heart. It was a sort of sweet hurtful ache. Jack was no Jack the Giant Killer. He never could be and I shouldn't have expected it. Like the rest of us, **Jack had his own preoccupations and troubles. I soon learned I had to use his strengths and overlook his limitations and his constant and increasing expectations of financial reward.**

Behind the scenes, things had taken a sharp detour from the incoherent, bumbling inaction of the afternoon. A new police e-mail advised me not to go down either route they had suggested the day before. Instead, "On the advice of our colleagues, we suggest you apply to the family court for a non-molestation order."

Non-Molestation Order

A non-molestation order as granted by a court is to protect the safety of the applicant from physical and mental abuse from the person who has abused him or her. It bars the abuser, whom the court terms the respondent, from coming near the applicant's home, communicating with him or her and also from getting his friends to harass or intimidate the applicant in any way. The time limit to the order may vary but, initially, twelve months is usual.

***

However, the cops' previous spoken advice not to let Red into the flat was still supposed to apply ahead of any court order. So was any plea from me to the police via a 999 phone call that was supposed to activate a "marker" within the police - *supposed to* as the operative phrase.

Some inner sense told me to draw my social worker into the loop. I was lucky that, when I phoned Gladys, she was in her office and that she answered my call. I think she was surprised, no, taken aback that I had taken my first timid steps to safety.

"Yes," Gladys answered my question about Red needing psychological counselling and domestic care, "we'll take care of Red, find him accommodation. He won't be homeless."

"Tonight," I insisted. "My safety has to start right now. There can't be half measures. Otherwise, it will damage my case or, worse, start Red's cycle of violence all over again."

"We'll find him somewhere. But for tonight, that's short notice as you must appreciate."

"You mean that tonight, it's a police cell."

"Yes," Gladys admitted with a guilty half voice.

Later while Jack and I were in my flat weighing up the options, Red turned up drunk. He couldn't manage the security code to get through the lobby on my floor. Jack immediately called the police on his cell phone and mentioned the "marker" we had been assured about the day before.

Two different police officers did respond, and

quickly. They were both experienced women who could see how drunk Red was. But they had no information, no inkling about the situation they had arrived to deal with. Can you imagine reducing the story you've read so far, if you're still with me, so that it's as concise and pithy as a telegram? I found it impossible, despite my advice in the previous chapter.

What came out of my lips was stuttering and incoherent. After all, there hadn't been time for me to start the court process for a non-molestation order. And Red was on the right floor but just outside the security door to the flat.

Jack came to my aid. But whereas Jack and I thought we were asking the police to prevent Red from getting back into the flat, the two women officers, new to my problem, thought this was some evenly balanced case and that their task was to be neutral. The officers shuttled between Red in the outer lobby and me in my flat.

"We've asked Red to stay overnight with one of his friends. He says he hasn't got any friends. Since we have to keep the two of you apart, we suggest you leave and that Red stays here in your flat."

I was dumbstruck. Let Red back in? Force me out? It seemed I would never get away from him and his violence. I could hardly believe what I was hearing. But I knew this was now or never. I had to stand my ground.

"This is my flat, my home. Look around you. See the damage to ornaments? All caused by Red. And what about him hitting me? No. It is for Red to leave. Earlier I phoned my social worker. She assured me that the city council would give him accommodation until the court case is decided. Red has his own social worker. He won't be homeless."

The officer drew breath at my sudden eloquence. But she had her answer.

"It's late. Social services will be closed. We'll take care of him tonight and see him on his way tomorrow."

A police cell; this was not what I wanted. And it was what I dreaded. It put me on the back foot and reduced my case so that Red could present himself as the injured party.

I didn't see the sadness that hit Red when he knew I was rejecting him. In fact, I don't think it hit him all at once. It dawned on him, tawdry episode by tawdry episode.

The next day the scenario repeated itself. Red spent the day drinking with his old soaks. But before Red tried to get back into the flat, I was confronted by a bevvy of police officers. There's no other word but *bevvy*. I wouldn't call it a posse but there were four of them. They arrived in hostile mode in the late afternoon.

A humorous writer could fashion a black comedy out of the scene. For these four officers were dancing a delicate balance between their socially acquired disdain of gays and their being forced to mouth politically correct words for their awkward treatment of a problematic case. It tested their duty to protect a vulnerable disabled person. And it made them uncomfortable.

There was the fit cop with the gym-toned physique and an English-Pakistani accent; two heavies, one with a heart, the other with a brain ready to follow orders at all costs; and a wiry policewoman determined to get noticed in the way she asserted herself.

To answer their enquiries, I repeated all over again what was now my catalogue of grievances. I was getting better at this because I was now more practised.

The fit cop wanted to ensure my answers protected the police's actions.

"Have you started court proceedings?"

"I've told the family court about my safety. [This was true; I had phoned them]. They're sending me forms to complete for a non-molestation order."

"So, you've started the process?"

"Yes."

That seemed to be the assurance he needed. If I had started with the courts, then that protected the police as well as me.

The policewoman was sitting on a formal dining chair. When there was a pause in the conversation, her chair creaked like a grasshopper on edge.

To add to the tension, the phone rang. I answered. It was something about the delivery of what I still called meals on wheels, one of the companies that delivered prepared meals to people, including older people, who preferred ready-made meals that could be heated in microwaves.

The phone rang again. And this time, unintentionally, Red's drunkenness had come to my aid, simply because he was phoning me from a pub, the Glass House nearby. The fit cop insisted on taking the call from me.

"It's Red," he said to all of us in the room, adding with surprise, "he's very intoxicated. Why," he continued to one of the heavies, "don't you go to him? He's in the Glass House across the road; explain to him that he can't come back here."

The heavy left.

Then the fit cop started to lecture me on what I could and couldn't do but he was interrupted by the phone ringing yet again. The wiry policewoman was having none of these continuous interruptions.

"Turn it off," she ordered me without her usual glacial smile.

"That's awkward for me. If I disconnect it, I may not be able to reconnect it when you've gone," I said.

She was having none of this, either. She stepped to the phone, yanked its cord out, resumed her stern seat on the formal dining chair, and recovered her frosty manner.

The fit cop started his lecture again as if I was a naughty schoolboy. He was interrupted, however, this time by the heavy cop, now back in the flat, who said, "I've spoken to Red. He won't be back tonight. Two of his friends have offered to put him up for the next few days. One said, 'We can't see him homeless.'"

"He's not homeless," I said. "I spoke to my social worker again today. They offered him somewhere to live and she told me he said no."

The fit cop then gave me more instructions. It sounded as if he was reading the riot act.

"Never let Red back into the flat. If he tries to get into the building, call 999 straight away. You need to take a proactive part in prevention. You need to change your telephone number; also, block his phone calls and his e-mails."

The cops trundled away, leaving me with the problem of reconnecting my landline phone.

***

Red sure liked his friends from two towns over, the more gregarious Tom with a failed marriage and five grown-up sons behind him and his older partner, Jerry, with a hardy, pinched face and ingenious skills with outsize plumbing pipes. Although Tom was a disabled fifty-year-old with a bulbous tummy caused by a double hernia, it was the older Jerry in his sixties who kept them both with his hard-earned and persistently hard-pressed work ethic.

They liked to let off steam in the big city once a week but, what with the vagaries of train services after 10.00 pm, no matter how drunk they were, they would stagger their way home to the boon-docks an hour earlier at 9.00 pm rather than risk being left out in the cold.

And it was back to their home that they took Red. They lived above a chippy and takeaway and had the flat to themselves every weekend until their landlord returned sharp as a tack each Monday.

Over the weekend Red could collapse onto the spare

bed chez Tom and Jerry. The days were a monotony of depression since Jerry was absent at work and Tom was absent in mind, oblivious to everything but continuous weed smoking. Neither Tom nor Jerry ever considered leaving their small town, never ventured very far afield and therefore never grew in their minds. On their flying visits to the city centre, you could take them out of their grotty suburbs but you couldn't take the small-minded suburbs out of them.

While he was with them, Red didn't dare say a word out of place but his mind worked overtime as he planned to get back into my flat by tugging my heartstrings. He knew he needed an ally. So, to this end, he programmed Tom.

"Blue will let me back if we soften him up. I know I can't stay here forever."

"We can't see you homeless," said complaisant Tom. "But the boss is back on Monday and needs his bed."

"That's the day I have to go back to hospital to have my dressings changed. I can't believe Blue would do this to me. I know I fucked up by getting drunk but he still has feelings for me. I'm sure of it. He can't leave me with nothing and no one."

"Why don't I phone Blue on Monday, tell him what train you'll arrive back home on and keep him informed of what happens on your way to hospital, while you're there, and when you leave? It'll be like a running commentary on BBC Sports Extra. Yes, Blue must still have feelings for you. He'll surely give in."

"That's what I hoped you'd say," agreed Red. "Cheers."

And that was what Tom did.

That Monday he phoned me to say Red had got off the train in town. He called me to say which bus Red took to the hospital. He phoned me when Red was in the outpatients' waiting room.

Each time I answered Tom politely but he guessed I wasn't going to budge or let Red come back.

"The police have told me not to," I said.

"Red says if he goes into rehab will you let him?"

"Rehab is what he should do but he will have to apply. Get his social worker to do it for him."

I wasn't being non-committal. I was beginning to feel more sure of myself since I now had a modicum of backup from the police.

3 LESSONS

1 One of the things I'd been thinking about was how experience, especially unhappy or bitter experience, changes us. It leaves its prickly mark on us because

our emotions are so raw. Yes, I'd been frightened by domestic abuse more than you can imagine. And even more frightened by the police's dire warning of imminent death.

2. So, when I thought about things with more perspective, I realised how Red's domestic abuse had itself manipulated me into a different state. To put it coarsely, it was like the way you could smell dog dirt on your shoe long after you've picked it up on the street, even after a nice soak in a bubble bath if you can afford such luxury. Or the way you might still feel a nasty scratch on the arm from an irate pussy whom you've tried to cuddle.

3. I vowed that these sour experiences would keep me on red alert from danger. Indeed, so had Red's domestic abuse. I wasn't going to put my head in that noose again if I could possibly help it.

***

Red arrived at the hospital where he was to have his dressings changed, out of breath, dirty, sweaty and exhausted.

"I'm sorry," he explained to the receptionist. "I know I'm a mess. My partner got the police to throw me out. I've nowhere to go. Can I wash first?" he asked with practised piteousness.

The flint-eyed receptionist was moved despite her experience of such cries. She directed him to the disabled toilet with its washbasin, soap and paper towels.

The nurse who treated Red's knee replaced his bandages with unfeeling professionalism. When she told him to rest, Red blurted out his story of woe.

"Wait with the other patients. We'll see what we can do."

Cautiously, Red took a pew. Whatever he thought inside, boiling with indignation and livid at me, he knew he had to act contrite as never before. He guessed that behind the scenes the desk staff were checking up on him and his story. After half an hour, when a staff member came over to him, he resumed his contrite expression as if his life depended on it.

"We've been in touch with social services. For tonight, we've arranged for you to go to this B&B. Here's the address and phone number. It's not too far to walk but we'll arrange an ambulance. Tomorrow, phone social services on this number. They'll arrange something more permanent for you then. You have a bus pass? Yes? Good."

Red heaved a breath of relief as if coming up for air after deep-sea diving. His mind was racing like a panicking horse in a steeplechase.

When the ambulance dropped him off that evening, he wasn't surprised that the hotel was dingy, the owner surly, and the room just short of squalid.

He clung to the red blanket on the bed as if it were a child's favourite toy. He slept fitfully and spoke in his dreams:

"Grandma, I'm suffocating I can't breathe. I don't want to die like this, alone in a slum B&B."

Red moved his fingers to scan the time on his phone and knocked a glass with water off the bedside table.

"I'm sorry about the glass," he cried, his eyes welling with tears, and speaking to the Indian owner as if he was there in the room. "But I can't pay for it. I have nothing. Please don't tell the hospital."

Red's breath was starting to whistle in his throat. He started to apologise to the hitherto non-present owner all over again when the said owner barged in without knocking.

"It's almost nine o'clock, my friend. Time to be up, out and away. You've got ten minutes," he rasped as if Red was the lowest scum he'd ever had to put up, though that couldn't possibly be true.

"Leave me alone," Red rasped back.

"What are you going to do if I persist, Rocket Man?"

the owner said tetchily.

The hotel receptionist, a young girl in a fetching sari, put her head around the door, and said perkily, "Is everything OK?"

"Everything is more than OK," retorted the owner. "It's bloody marvellous."

The girl rolled her eyes. She'd heard it all before. The owner turned back on Red.

"You've got five. The clock's ticking. I'm waiting."

With that, he smiled, a glacial grin that would curdle any curry.

Red said, "I'm in pain. I've just had a double operation on my knee."

"You're not in pain. You're not even ill," said the dry-as-dust-in-your throat smile. "You're a malingerer."

"I have been ill, in hospital two weeks. I've nowhere to go."

"That's what they all say. And among the nowhere to go to places is my hotel. If you're not out in ten minutes, the police will be here to help you on your way."

The owner fairly slammed the door.

Red wanted to yelp but what was the point? There was a hesitant knock on the door and the young girl came in cautiously.

"We have to be quick. The boss has gone out for his paper. He'll be back momentarily."

Her voice sounded educated and caring.

"Social services sent you, didn't they? They're on the phone for you in the lobby. I think they've got directions for where you're to go next. Please hurry. You don't want to miss this call."

Indeed, the call from social services told Red where to go and what to say, and how to register.

When Red arrived at Milton Meadow Hotel, the so-called hotel social services had found for him, a surly receptionist took him outside the main building to show him his room in the hotel annexe.

He looked around, fearful yet intensely curious. The first thing he noticed was how dry and musty the air was.

"No one's opened a window in here for quite some time," he thought. "Cripes. Nobody's even breathed in here for a long time unless it was to croak their last. I wonder how many poor souls died here. Will I be the next? Christ, I hope not."

But at least Red knew that this was going to be some sort of home until he thought I would give in and let him move back into our flat. However, Milton Meadow Hotel looked bleak, smelt bleak, and seemed to be telling him, "We will bury you here."

His designated room in the hotel annexe sure was cold, damn cold, freezing in fact. The old navy-blue blanket wasn't enough. You could die of cold here and no one would give a damn. How could I do this to him, ignore his birthday, ignore Christmas and New Year, and leave him to rot in the middle of a pandemic without presents and treats and without any true friends to rescue him?

That first night when he put out the light, Red was afraid things might somehow get into his room. What things? He wasn't sure. But things with tentacles. Locking the door wasn't enough to stop them. He heard things he couldn't identify talking and laughing in the next room. It was all hairy and the hairy things could sure squeeze in through cracks and the gap between the door in its frame and the rough wood floor beneath. In Red's frightened state he thought these hateful things had eyes that could tell what he had done wrong in his life. All he wanted was to escape.

Red knew he was sweating like mad. He could feel sweat trickling down from his forehead, matting his hair, and greasing his armpits. From the room next door, he heard shrieking laughter again. He froze, thinking that if he moved, he would scream.

Silence.

Next day back downtown Red couldn't wait to tell everyone in the bars his side of things. His first targets were Phil and Tony Tracker, a pair of lifelong bachelors who regularly propped up the front bar in the Glass House.

"We've been together twenty years," Red began. "I gave up everything for him, family, flat, pets. And he treats me like this. But I haven't given up. We've had our ups and downs and he's always wanted me back. The flat's my forever home."

The Trackers' response astonished Red. After their tut-tutting, Phil said,

"This is a small town. You're no angel. Simply pass what's happened around and, through the right people, you'll get someone else and a home as well. You up for another whisky chaser?"

***

The next day when I phoned my social worker and told her about the police interrogation when four of them had burst in on me, she replied,

"Don't concern yourself with Red's future. We've got him a place in a hotel. I can't tell you where. It's secure accommodation. He will be safe. Concentrate on your own future."

Of course, that wasn't the end or the swift route to the court. Gladys Knowles had admitted that Red was in some B&B, unnamed to me but a hotel nevertheless.

And once Red was in the B&B, if not settled there, he got back into my building, into the upper lobby by my flat and passed a note under the door:

"Blue, please talk to me. I'm lonely, confused. It's all I deserve. I'm in rehab as you wanted. Red, XXX."

Shortly afterwards, he sent a letter through the Post Office.

"Blue, I know in your heart after loving you 20 years, I'm sure you still love me. I'm in rehab as you asked. I cannot drink here at all. I know we have problems but I've never cheated. Please don't hurt me. I will always love you and miss doing things with you. You can call me to see how I'm coping. Very alone and depressed. Nothing left now. You asked me to do this for our relationship.

"Reza [his social worker] knows I've not eaten for 1 week. Can't cope on my own, need company. Please, you've got my number. Call me so you know I'm OK! We've had our arguments, ups and downs, but I would not do this to you. Please help me. We will get through this. Please reply. Love always, Red."

He certainly knew how to bring sadness, even anguish, to his unhappy plight. Of course, I was more than touched, moved by this piteous letter but I was also suspicious. Yes, I knew Red always had problems coping on his own. But was he really in rehab? Had I ever said if he went into rehab this would save our relationship?

My only way of getting any concrete information about Red's supposed rehab was from Gladys, my social worker. Her principal answer was just as I suspected,

"No, Red is not in rehab. You have to apply for that, get on a list and wait your turn 'till there's a vacancy. The hotel will have a no-drink or drugs policy but that is different from a 24/7 rehab program."

Her reply partly eased my conscience but the other voice in my ear was that of the first police officers who had come to the flat,

"Domestic abuse may start with minor incidents. But if it isn't checked it will grow. Take action now. You don't want to end up on a mortuary slab."

Whatever crises I went through, whatever hurdles the system set on my path to get a non-molestation order, this police voice in my ear remained loud and clear like a trumpet voluntary. I mustn't waver.

I knew that was good and sound advice. But I wasn't free from Red and his needling by any manner of means.

As you know, I had told the police I had begun court proceedings. Yes, this was true, indeed I had. But don't for a moment think as I did at my most naïve, that this meant I had done the hardest part by opening up about my distress to the police and followed their advice that everything was going to be smooth sailing from now on. Far from it.

I had more than my fair share of well-wishers telling me that Red was nice, loyal, a good fellow, a good egg, or whatever.

What I should have said to them was simply that abusers show a different face to the world. Can someone still be "nice" if they murder their partner or children? The fact is that I didn't dare to answer Red's fan club base.

Nor did I know then that all the time, underneath the surface the legal machinery existed that could show me the way to get help.

Here are some of the mechanisms, based on information on government websites:

Protection and Police Safety Orders

The Domestic Violence Act 1995 marked a new era in dealing with family violence when it came into force on

1 July 1996. It is now the primary legal weapon for fighting family violence. It overhauled the Domestic Protection Act 1982 and set out how victims of family violence could obtain protection orders. It amended the Guardianship Act 1968, tightening its guardianship and custody provisions, giving children greater safety, particularly if allegations of domestic violence were made in custody and access cases.

Not one of the agencies or authorities I went to for help mentioned this law and how it might apply to me.

ADVICE

Life is full of contradictions. As a retired conductor of opera told me fifty years ago, "Life isn't meant to be easy."

If we think about the self-serving social platitudes of comfort and consolation, such as, "When you fall in love, it will be forever," the old conductor's bitter remark cuts through from illusion to reality. Thus, "Life isn't meant to be easy," is one of the bargains that life surely keeps. Though you may not think this when you are twenty, by the time you are thirty with all the different experiences of your previous ten years, you can see and test the truth of the old conductor's words.

So, here my double-edged advice is contradictory.

2 Contradictions

1 In your need to escape your tormentor, if you have found a true ally, a helper, within your family or workmates or outside, use him or her to the utmost until you have reached your goal of freedom. This also applies if your helper works for one of the professional services, police, social work or the NHS. This does not mean that he or she won't have their own motives for helping you. But to use another metaphor, we have to play with the cards we've got.

2 We like to believe the concluding upbeat anthem of genius show creators Rodgers and Hammerstein in their immortal musical, *Carousel*, that when you walk through a storm if you hold your head up high (etc.), you will never walk alone. When Liverpudlian pop stars Gerry Marsden and the Pacemakers made their deliberately voice-of-the-people version in the 1960s and scored their third successive Number One hit in the UK charts, they certainly amplified the traditional, wholesome and comforting interpretation as Liverpool football fans turned the *Carousel* song into a football anthem.

But if you listen with your mind as well as your ears to the show as a whole, it carries an opposite meaning to the shibboleth of you'll never walk alone.

Carousel is in a line of masterpieces of musical theatre, including Monteverdi's *The Coronation of Poppea*, Verdi's *La Traviata*, and Puccini's *Madama Butterfly*, where you can go, love and be swamped by the procession of adorable melodies and discover that the show is telling you something different from what you imagined. All these shows may change your mind about something you never challenged before.

We are individuals and, in the end, we always have to walk alone. So, if you feel trapped and violated, what you most need if you are ever to escape your tormentor, is persistence and stamina. I know, it is often hard to keep going.

Some people reading this may think this is the easy advice of someone outside my situation. But, in fact, I lived for too long under domestic abuse and it was stamina that got me through its excesses. I think I know what I'm talking about. This book is a by-product of bitter experience.

EPISODE 6

Specific Overtures?

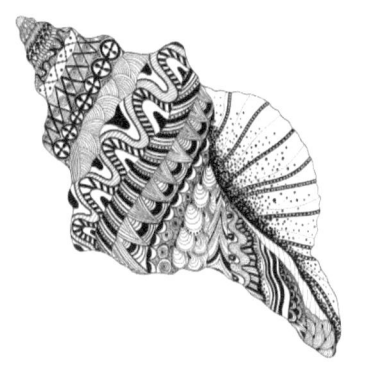

Once I caught sight of the shore to safety ahead of unceasing troubled waters, my first hurdle came with completing the family court application form for a non-molestation order. My ability to read via Braille is poor. As a visually impaired applicant, my preferred format was and is large print.

Law requires all agencies, educational institutions and business companies to provide printed material in large print when users need it. Surely a court would. But no, at first the court could not or simply did not.

After a delay to mull things over, the court did provide the form in large print and sent it to me. The application consisted of personal details such as name, address, etc., a brief declaration about the abuse you have suffered, which remedy you seek and a synopsis of your experience with some details. I had already been working on my synopsis. With every setback along the court's tortuous path, I refined it by shortening my paragraphs and sharpening my meaning.

The process then asked you, the applicant, to submit the form, not to your local court but to an address in Slough. I did so and waited for some response or at least an acknowledgement. I sent off the packet by recorded delivery and waited. I waited and waited but answer came there none over the next fortnight. Various phone calls to my local family court yielded nothing but inaccurate counselling.

After two weeks, it seemed everything I had done had miscarried in the mail. That's putting it politely. It was certainly lost. And my local court had no provision to call the mysterious department in Slough. The court told me that inter-court communication was strictly by e-mail and, apparently, ineffective.

So, we, the family court and I had to start again. First, the court asked me to submit an online form to its own local offices. It was difficult for me to complete the online form, which I couldn't see properly but I did my best. When I submitted the form, it arrived at the family court with the questions clear as daylight but all my typed answers washed away in the ether.

We started all over again with another paper form, which did arrive at the court. However, some court officer returned the completed form with a snooty note:

"You haven't completed the first page with your contact details. Without them, the court can't process your application."

I hadn't done so because the court had a provision for contact details to be submitted on a separate sheet, which I had done. This was to conceal my new phone number from Red. I wanted to say, but didn't, that the snooty court official had no difficulty in returning the form to me at my correct address.

Four weeks had passed since my initial approach to the court. By now the court secretariat was ready for a major compromise. Since the court was only a thirty-minute walk from my home, Mr Brown of the court (that's not his real name), suggested I take the completed and mistakenly returned form back to the court and ask permission from security at the front door to hand it personally to him in his office on the 11th floor.

This was so that the case could be heard urgently the next day. The court secretariat understood that the failed application process had taken its toll on my nerves and their patience.

Gladly I walked to the court through mild rain. It was lunchtime. When I arrived, I was turned away. In the way stood Humbug 2020. The security guardian of the threshold, a man clinically obese twice over, declared that,

"This Mr Brown, whom you say is the court manager, doesn't exist. There are too many court officers named Brown for me to check without more precise information. I'm not letting you in. And neither will anyone else."

From his point of view, he, the surly guardian of the threshold, had spoken and that was that.

It is a sad consequence of the insidious English class system that if any organisation gives an undereducated yob, especially a middle-aged yob, some authority, it creates a mini-Hitler, eager to forget discretion and ready to use his puny power to the detriment of smooth security. This was yet another impasse I had to face. But I had to stand my ground as never before, lurking in the rain and hoping that an intelligent and caring person would turn up and help me.

My aggravation and patience were rewarded. Another authoritative figure, senior to the first and himself skulking in the background during his lunch break but still inside the court building and out of the rain, acknowledged that he knew all about Mr Brown's instructions regarding me. He sent me to the appropriate higher floor for Mr Brown.

Mr Brown himself did not appear, perhaps because, through no fault of my own, I was now over an hour late. However, one of his juniors did receive me and, at my suggestion, she read my application just in case there was a mistake of some sort.

At last, all was well.

This junior also advised me about applying for an

extension to the non-molestation order in a year and what my second synopsis should cover then. I ask you readers to keep this in mind for when we get to 2021.

You might think the topsy turvy progress to getting a court hearing before a judge for the non-molestation order was simply an example of government circumlocution: going round and round in circles to get something done, an uphill struggle but with a predictable ending, success.

3 Recommendations for the Court

1 Always have to hand copies of various court application forms print-ready from a computer in Braille and large print, besides those in regular print in English and other languages widely used across England.
2 Train all security guards, receptionists and bailiffs and officers of the court in common courtesy; forbid sub-Hitler attitudinising.
3 Ensure safety procedures and due electronic processes so that citizen's documents do not disappear into the bowels of the mysterious, all-consuming Slough repository.

***

Court mishaps were one problem and impersonal. But what made my route to safety via the family court tortuous and unsettling were the hazards of keeping Red at bay, out of my home and out of sight until the official hearing.

Red's latent offstage threats were a continuous reminder of his skill at irritation. You might think he had a bad hand of cards but with dexterous play, he almost came up trumps.

First, came a phone call from his friend, Tom, from above the chippy:

"Can you pack a bag with his clothes? Red only has the clothes he was wearing when the police took him away, shorts and an old top. It's too cold for just that."

"Yes, sure. I'll do that but who will come and collect them? Red isn't allowed back here."

The phone went dead.

But when I looked at my PC, there were two e-mail messages from Red:

"Why Blue, can't I have 5 mins talk on the phone? I deserve that at least. I've not eaten for 2 days. Please, if you still have some feelings, speak to me, Blue.

"I need to know why you can do this after 20 years. I've gave up everything for you. I don't deserve to be homeless, what with pandemic, etc. Please talk to me. I need you. Don't do this to us. I've no one, nothing."

Of course, I knew what Red was trying to do with his mix of wheedling, reproaches, and heart-tugging. It wasn't that I was in danger of falling for his pleading. My memories of his physical attacks were too recent and too raw. But I recognised, as always, that this was a fallible human being, someone not good at dealing with his emotions and, as usual, relying on others to help screen out his practical problems.

Over the next two days, I sorted through Red's clothes, shoes and personal items, washed and dried the clothes and packed everything carefully into an imitation leather holdall. Then I waited.

There were more e-mail messages from Red:

"Blue, I love you. Give me a chance. I will prove I can be the person you want. Show me you're the man I fell in love with."

And:

"Why, Blue? Don't block my number. I'm sorry. I miss you. I won't call unless you keep in touch. Love, Red."

I should have paid immediate attention to the third message. It had a heavy hint:

"Blue, the scar on my leg has come open. It's

bleeding. I can't get a doctor down here. Please if you've still got some love for me."

A day later, Red appeared in the lobby outside the flat. His aim was to reproach me, to make me feel guilty, and needle his way with an excuse back into the apartment.

"I had nowhere to go," he began. "While I stayed with Tom after the police let me out of the cell, I felt so alone. Tom's partner was at work during the day and Tom just filled in his time smoking weed and getting depressed. They couldn't let me stay there permanently. You know they live above a fish and chip shop and they only have the place to themselves at weekends. On the Monday I came back into town and went to hospital to have my dressings changed. You know that as well. But I had nowhere to go."

Then Red told me his version of the first hotel that I've already described.

"Seeing I was desperate, the hospital arranged for me to stay in a bed and breakfast hotel nearby. Grubby place. My room had a broken window and a blanket that didn't even cover the bed. The next morning the owner, Indian, we weren't far from the Asian neighbourhood, wanted me out pronto. He woke me at eight in the morning and told me to get up and go immediately. The receptionist was his daughter. She took pity on me. When he was out, she made some toast for me in their breakfast room. You could tell how dirty it was. There was a bug with bulging eyes on the table. It lurched onto my plate and mounted the slice of buttered toast. I tried to bat away the bug on the slice of toast. It clung onto the toast then scrambled into the compost waste bin. It was like it was rearing to get in, breed, and come back to haunt the hotel guests."

I didn't know Red could be so inventive. But all I said was, "I think you're exaggerating."

"Am I? You go there and see for yourself."

"What happened next?"

"The girl phoned social services, or maybe they phoned her. Anyway, they put me up in Milton Meadow Hotel."

"And?"

"It's meant to be a hotel but it's clearly a doss house. I'm staying in the annexe, round the corner from the main building. It's freezing cold. The other people there are all youngsters. They're on weed, smoking all the time and talking about when they're going to get high again. There's supposed to be food in the kitchen, packaged meals, but these young kids grab it all. There's nothing left."

I managed not to let Red get further in my building than the upstairs lobby, not into the flat. I showed him the bag with his clothes.

"I've got everything ready for you, toiletries as well."

"It's too heavy. I can't carry that. My leg's not strong enough."

I had managed to get into the flat, keep the door locked and alert the police but, when I looked back in the lobby, Red had gone. The police turned up, a mature policewoman and a younger man who said, "I've called for an ambulance for paramedics to look at Red's leg."

The woman said, "I'll take the holdall with Red's clothes to the main police station. He can collect them there. This way it takes away any excuse for him to come back here. If he does come back, call the police immediately."

Just as things got quiet, an ambulance arrived with two experienced paramedics. Now there was no one here for them to treat since Red had gone but I felt duty-bound to let them into the flat so that I could explain things. They seemed fascinated by my convoluted story. When I finished, the man said, "Don't let Red back in."

Just then the intercom buzzer sounded so loud as to awaken the dead. It was like the clarion trumpets in the song, 'Goldfinger.' from the movie. I suppose that was my nerves squealing. I looked at the little intercom screen in the hall. Red was on the front doorsteps. This gave the paramedics a reason to leave and examine him downstairs. After ten minutes they rang the buzzer.

"We've changed Red's dressing down here on the street. Everything is fine with his knee. It's improving. Red's gone now. But, again, let us warn you for your own safety, not to let Red back in."

The paramedics left.

Then another posse of police arrived to check for my safety. When I explained that the ambulance crew had done their work and had now gone, the lead cop said, "I arranged for the ambulance to come. When I knew it wasn't necessary, I forgot to cancel it. How's progress with the non-molestation order?"

"It's hardly progressing. It's one muddle and dead-end after another."

"The main thing is that you've started things. That's all you can do. But keep us in the loop about the actual process."

I didn't breathe a sigh of relief. I was spaced out and no mistake.

***

Meanwhile, Red was living in acute dismay. In his fevered state, everything in the loathsome room in the dilapidated hotel annexe was turning blood-red. It seemed blood was pattering down from the loft just above him and ending in a prickly shower above his washbasin. Blood everywhere. And never a drop to drink. When he pulled the sheet farther up the bed, he thought blood from the jagged glass he had used to threaten me some time ago was now running down between his knuckles. His teeth felt as if they were crunching razor blades.

Red couldn't stop remembering the past, what was and what might have been but never what he had done wrong. Sometimes he thought his fond memories would drive him mad. When he was alone, which he hated, he would clench his fists into a tight grip, trying to keep himself fixed to the spot to prevent being buffeted by blustery winds coming through gaps in the rickety window frames. He was afraid of flying away in a gale and getting scattered in pieces.

Red remembered me off on one of my scholarly tangents talking about the domino theory as it applied to satellite Communist countries in eastern Europe after World War II and to struggling post-colonial countries in South East Asia during America's war in Vietnam.

What I had tried to teach him was:

"Sometimes it's like this domino theory in our ordinary lives. Yes, events are like dominoes. When a first domino knocks over a second domino, the second knocks over the third. And so on."

Red could now relate this to his recent life: getting so drunk that he got himself attacked and badly injured; being rude to the people in the hospital and really nasty to me; getting even more drunk every day after the hospital discharged him; trashing me and trashing his own life.

At that point, Red stopped thinking. He didn't want to follow his thoughts through to any logical conclusion. But he couldn't stop hearing my words about the way everything ended up in the domino theory, "Everything flattened, destroyed."

He might be disintegrating but, Red kept repeating to himself, he had means of escape. He was allowed out of the hotel in the day and with his precious bus pass truly now his most treasured possession, he could get to me.

Thus encouraged, Red made a second attempt to reinstate himself in my flat. This time he was more intrusive and might have been successful. It was way more disturbing than his first attempt.

Every other Tuesday morning, Edna, a dear sweet

person, came early to clean the floors in my flat. Deft with a vacuum cleaner that looked like a Dalek from BBC's *Doctor Who*, mop and bucket and plenty of detergent, she could get carpet and laminate so clean that, yes, you could eat your dinner off the floor. Just before Edna arrived, however, I had to prepare the way.

The polite way to describe my flat would be to say it was overcrowded. House Doctor would have a field day of decluttering, perhaps eliminating bookcases, furniture, and kitchen items spilling from the diminutive so-called bistro kitchen into the interconnected lounge. Anyway, many of these would be far too heavy to expect a cleaner to move. So, each evening before Edna arrived, I moved such items as suitcases, plastic boxes, etc. into the lobby just beyond my front door.

Red knew what I did and when I did it and he timed his unwanted re-entry perfectly to coincide with the few moments when my front door was ajar. Before I knew it, he was inside, plonked on what was his sofa, the one with a wooden frame, false leather brown upholstery and cushions of corduroy beige, a settee that he had bought via hire purchase.

Just then, Edna arrived.

I faced a double dilemma: try and call the police and risk Red tearing the phone out; or try to placate Red so as not to scare Edna. So, which was more important? Keeping Edna onside and not frightened with the faint hope of extricating Red? Which had priority? My safety or making sure I kept a good cleaner? If you have a nice home and a reliable cleaner, you know the answer.

The other voice in my ear was that of the first police officers who had come to the flat:

"Domestic abuse may start with minor incidents. But if it isn't checked it will grow. Take action now. You don't want to end up on a mortuary slab."

In my head, I repeated my core belief for survival like a religious mantra. Whatever crises I went through, whatever hurdles the court system set on my path to get a non-molestation order, this police voice in my ear remained loud and clear like a reliably insistent trumpet voluntary. I knew I mustn't waver.

What I did the day Red got into the flat was to parry Red until Edna had finished and I could get help. The one thing I knew I mustn't do was have a verbal and physical row and scare Edna away. I was so anxious I felt sure I must be mentally ill. Red, of course, had plenty to say.

"The two women who changed my dressings here came to the B&B. But no one else will help me. Social services is just like Bojo the Clown, promises more than delivers."

All this chatter was while Edna was cleaning the floors of the flat. I was on tenterhooks, not wanting to give the slightest hint that the little scene was the unwanted aftermath of domestic abuse. When Edna had gone, Red made it clear he wanted to stay. All I could do was field his verbal flourishes trying to weaken me. Whatever he thought, I wasn't going to give in. But I didn't know how I could get out of the situation intact.

Red said as if hinting, "The house rule where I am is I have to be back by ten o'clock. Otherwise, I can't go back there."

Was he fishing to stay in the flat until it was too late for him to get back to the transients' hotel? Everything I did that morning was to keep him calm. I didn't dare phone for help. Nor did I want to provoke him into destroying the phone.

I pushed my glasses higher on the bridge of my nose to scrutinise Red better. Blood was seeping through Red's knee dressing like a magician's surprise, ugly, unquenchable. I tore up a pillowcase to bandage the knee then **I made him a cup of tea.**

While he was drinking it, I opened my PC in the bedroom and typed an e-mail to neighbour Jack Rascal asking him to meet me in the nearby cafe. I told Red I had to go out briefly. He rose as if to remonstrate. I looked hard at him and said, "Please don't start again."

He subsided.

When I got to the coffee shop, trembling slightly, I ordered a cappuccino for Jack and an American for me.

Jack appeared, his face a mix of getting angry and being perturbed.

Before I could say anything, Jack said, "Red is back in your flat. I called you and he picked up the phone. He said 'Hello.' I recognised his voice and put down my phone. So, what's up?"

When I got through my lamentable tale, he said abruptly and ultra-efficiently, "We've got to stop this straight away. I'll call the police."

He moved to a quiet corner of the cafe, starting to speak on his mobile phone. When he came back to the table, he said, "The police will be there shortly."

I wasn't shaking visibly. But Jack sensed my inner agitation. His phone rang. He turned away to take the call, then turned back to me, "The police are in your flat. They need you to go back there, to speak to them and explain the situation. It's your property. They can't act without you being there."

Jack knew my agitation was worsening, a sickening sort of psychological fear.

"I know you're apprehensive but, if the police are there, Red can't hurt you. Do you want me to come with you? I can stay right outside just in case."

"Thank you but no. As always, you've been a great help but I've got to face this. I don't want to. I believed the police when they told me just a few weeks ago that Red wouldn't come back. I shouldn't have trusted them. I'll call you when it's over - if it ever is."

As I left him, I knew he was eyeing me as I made a physical effort to control myself.

I returned to my flat swaying although I hadn't had anything more than coffee. I went straight to the bedroom, avoiding the main room where the policewomen were.

One came into the bedroom to question me. She seemed familiar if not with my particular story, then with the general pattern of domestic abuse. After I explained how Red had got into the flat, she only had two questions.

"Given what you've just told me, why did you make him a brew? You make it look as if you were welcoming him back."

"That wasn't the reason. His getting into the flat while I was making everything ready for the cleaner put me into a strange situation. I didn't want to upset Edna in any way. I couldn't leave. I had to parry his visit and make sure he didn't damage the phone and leave me isolated. It's only because I have one friend outside but near at hand that you're here."

"Are you ready to speak to Red?"

"No. I'm too scared. And I don't want to compromise the situation any further."

"What do you want us to do?"

"Please take him back to his hotel."

And so, the police officers took Red back through the hall. He called out for all the world to hear, "I love you, Blue."

This did not staunch my fears but, with Red away, I had some respite.

Red wasn't going to take his second ejection from the flat calmly. A few days later I received his riposte in a letter sent through the regular mail:

"Blue,

"Why do a dirty trick like you did? If you asked me to leave I would of. To try to save our relationship but you called the police. I Done nothing wrong.

"I thought we was talking through things.

"I'm stuck on my own through lockdown and our 20th anniversary. I've got nothing. Lost everything. Gave it all up to be with you. But all you can do is hurt me and talk to Jack behind my back. More than 2 in this relationship.

"I will never stop loving you. We could of worked this out some way. Please don't tell me you haven't feelings for me after so long.

"Please reply if that's the only way you want us to.

"Love always, Red."

He wasn't an experienced writer, far from it. Yet his words came at me from his raw experiences, characterised and weighted with an emotional thrust wholly out of the ordinary. My "dirty trick" was less than his in getting into the flat. I knew I mustn't put myself in a position where he could hurt me physically ever again.

Red's next prong of attack was another flurry of e-mails, again to tug at my better feelings, if not my heartstrings. This time it was a cascade of pleas via e-mails.

"Please Blue, help me, no one else is. I don't know what to do."

"Please call me, Blue. I love you. I need to talk. Why have you done this to us?"

If Red's intention was to make me feel like a heel, then he failed. Nevertheless, the continuous barrage of pleas and reproofs shook me to the core, like turning my spine to ice. I couldn't help feeling compassionate. The police had urged me, no, ordered me, to block Red's e-mails. But I'm not a computer wiz and it was some time before, by a process of trial and error, that I succeeded in blocking the pesky e-mails just as the police had insisted all along.

One productive consequence of Red getting into my flat was that it provided me with more information for my summary of domestic abuse for the family court.

As to that summary, you know the gruesome details of Red's physical attacks and psychological warfare. This is part of what I wrote:

"The triggers for Red's violence are excessive drinking that leads to Tourette syndrome-type verbal abuse and continues with physical assault e.g.: blows to my testicles; twisting my wrists - I have osteoarthritis - and hitting me with TV remotes and plates thrown with or without food; also, lobbing fruit. He spits at me and on carpets and furniture. You can see the scars where he slammed a door onto my left hand.

"He also and deliberately broke the glass of three pictures when he was in a rage; damaged my *Wireless for the Blind* by throwing it about; destroyed a drawer in a small chest; and (earlier) destroyed a telephone connection.

"His psychological abuse is often harder to take for, while the violence is sporadic, Red's continuous taunts about my eyesight; his forcing me to do menial tasks on my hands and knees, picking up crumbs of food while ridiculing me, is gross. This he does whether sober or drunk, constantly belittling me.

"I have lived in constant fear. I can't see where blows are coming from. The expletives are degrading, being called an 'old blind cunt,' [etc.], over and over again.

"I have tried years of kindness and support through Red's travails with benefit problems. He blames me for the UK government moving disabled people such as him from moderate DLA to far less PIP. He blames me for his separation from his family even though I gave him a home when his original council made him homeless.

"He has threatened me with major repercussions when he is better, recovered from recent knee surgery.

"I ask for the court's protection."

Five weeks after police had taken Red away and after a month of mishaps with my application, the family court heard the application and adjudicated. Five weeks! I can't pretend that it seemed like five years but it certainly felt like five months given the papers required by the court from me; papers that then had to be written again when they were mislaid; and the psychological turmoil in my own troubled frame of mind.

Because of Covid restrictions, the court hearing was held in what they termed a Phone Meet with the judge speaking from his home to me in mine. He tried to be charming, to put me at my ease with such pleasantries as "I see from your age that you are due your first Covid vaccine very soon. I envy you because I have to wait another month for mine."

Because the hearing had been labelled *Urgent* and the paperwork had been refined as if with a fine-toothed comb, the case was now straightforward enough. The judge granted the non-molestation order for twelve months, subject to confirmation or revision by a second judge at a second hearing where the respondent (Red) could challenge the order.

I quote much of the order since this may help future victims of abuse see how the court discharges its verdict and why.

Non-Molestation Order, Edited Sample

The order, a public document sent via bailiffs to Red at his temporary address and to me via e-mail, read:

"Deputy District Judge XXX, sitting at the Family Court, considered an application for an order made by the Applicant without notice to the Respondent and heard the Applicant who stated that: i. The content of his statement is true; ii. There had been a delay in making the application because he had initially tried to issue it online but this, for some reason, had been ineffective; iii. The Respondent had lived with him for about three years although they had known each other for a much longer period; iv. The Respondent was removed from the Applicant's home and has since then been accommodated by the City Council;

"v. The Respondent has, until recently, continued to harass the Applicant by telephone as a result of which the Applicant has been forced to change his telephone number. On one occasion the Respondent entered the Applicant's apartment in the wake of the cleaner who attends periodically and had to be removed.

"vi. There would be no need for the Respondent to come within 100 metres of the Applicant's home but he [the Applicant - me] accepts that there is some clothing of the Respondent still there together with documents [such as]: 2 the Respondent's passport and there are also some items of furniture and equipment which the Applicant accepts belong to the Respondent. In relation to these, the Applicant indicates that he is happy to release these to a third party by prior arrangement without the attendance of the Respondent.

"And Ordered That: 1) From and after the time when the Respondent is made aware of the terms of this Order whether in writing (by any means whether paper or electronic) or telephone or otherwise the Respondent (whether by himself or acting jointly with any other person) must not: a) Use or threaten any violence towards the Applicant; b) Come within 100 metres of the Applicant's home; c) Intimidate, harass or pester the Applicant; d) Send any threatening or abusive messages to the Applicant, whether by letter, text, email or any other form of written communication; e) Publish any form of information about the Applicant on or by social media including but not limited to Facebook, WhatsApp, Snapchat; f) Communicate with the Applicant whether by letter, telephone, text message or other means of communication; g) Damage or attempt to damage or threaten to damage any property belonging to the Applicant or jointly owned by the parties; h) Damage or attempt to damage or threaten to damage any of the contents of the Apartment aforesaid;

"2) The Respondent must not instruct nor encourage any other person to do anything which he is forbidden to do by the terms of this Order;

"3) This Order will remain in force until 4.00 pm on

[date given] or further Order of the Court;

"4) The Court will reconsider the application and whether the Order should continue at a further hearing before a Deputy District Judge with an estimated length of hearing 30 minutes. This hearing will take place remotely by telephone conference and further directions about that hearing are set out below;

"5) If a party does not participate in that hearing, Court may make an Order including a final order in his/her absence. 6) The attendance of the Applicant if legally represented may be excused providing instructions can be given by telephone."

The order did allow for Red to make a contrary statement at a subsequent hearing:

"9) If the Respondent wishes to oppose the application, he must tell the court and the Applicant before the next hearing. He must do that by preparing a witness statement setting out his version of the events referred to in the Applicant's statement, and must send copies of his statement by email to the court and to the Applicant/Applicant's solicitors so that the copies are received at least 48 hours before the hearing."

There would be no costs incurred.

The judge and the court had made the order without reference to Red because, with all the delays in getting the application to the court and any implied danger to me, the matter had become urgent. Therefore,

"11) This Order is made without notice to the Respondent because the Court was satisfied that it was just and convenient to make the order without notice, having had regard to all the circumstances of the case including in particular: a) The risk of significant harm to the applicant attributable to conduct of the respondent, if the order is not made immediately; b) That it is likely that the applicant will be deterred or prevented from pursuing the application if an order is not made immediately; and c) The Applicant's vulnerability as a partially sighted person. In making this order the court made no findings of fact and considered sections 45(1) and (2) of the Family Law Act 1996."

Both Red and I received our copies of the order. As specified above, Red was to be allowed an opportunity to reply at a subsequent hearing. The court order told him:

"If you think the Order should be set aside or varied you may apply for this at the hearing provided for below. At the hearing, the court will hear from both parties and decide whether to confirm, or vary, or set aside the Order or give directions for a further hearing."

Accordingly, the court held its second hearing at

which Red as respondent could offer his response, make a counterclaim or simply have his say. Although the hearing was supposed to happen within two weeks, it was three weeks before it took place, again by telephone. Red did not acknowledge receipt of the non-molestation order, nor did he make himself available for this telephone hearing.

At this second hearing, a different judge proved as patient and considerate as the first:

"These are strange times. I'm calling you from my kitchen."

This gave me something to think about: an old-fashioned kitchen with a roaring fire and a mighty Aga for cooking? A scullery in a Victorian house with a breakfast room attached? An ultra-modern chrome and marble hall with an island as centrepiece? Or maybe just a peninsula?

But the judge's only question was, "Were you and the respondent friends or in a relationship?"

I answered straightforwardly, "Both, but sometimes one and sometimes the other."

I could see why the distinction was important from the court's point of view but, to me, violence was as bad in one case as the other, unless your interpretation of the violence was that it was likely to be more damaging within a relationship rather than among quarrelling friends.

I was thinking, "I've been reading Lawrence Durrell's Alexandria books. He makes one of his characters say something like, 'The human heart is a medical condition. There isn't a remedy or a cure.' I think we all know what he's getting at."

Anyway, the second judge confirmed the original order.

How did Red take this? Over the years Red had created his personal image of me, boasting about me and my writing when I wasn't there, ridiculing me in public before his drink-addled friends. After the court hearings were over, I understood that, from Red's point of view, only when his image of me was complete did he see it disintegrate, vanish into thin air, or, more prosaically, discover it had been taken from him as if by some mysterious force. In reality, it was by his own stupid actions.

How Does What I Have Written Apply to You?

Try to think you are on a particular journey, not that your problems will be resolved in one fell swoop by the police or the courts.

Have you ever wondered how actors in a play learn

and know their lines? I have. I've also wondered how soloists in a concert of classical music at the front of the stage and without the score in front of them know the right notes in the right order and can then interpret the music.

I asked a classical pianist how he did it. He said, "I learn the music in stages, stages that are like the stops on the London Underground, the Tube, or the subway in New York 'where the people ride in a hole in the ground.' Each section has its destination title, like Piccadilly or Leicester Square. By building your knowledge in blocks through known signposts you make the score more digestible and less overwhelming because you focus on smaller sections."

4 Stages on Your Route to Freedom

And this is how any of you who are victims of domestic abuse or victim helpers can interpret your journey.

1 Your first stage comes when you decide to take action and find a friend, family member, or someone in medicine, social services, or police who will help you. Of course, since you are still on an uncharted journey you don't have the advantage of reading a map to the London Underground or New York subway but, then, you don't have as many stops to

learn and negotiate.

If you have escaped your tormentor's home, that is a crucial stage.

2 But you are best advised to secure your safety through one of the non-violence orders discussed in Episode 5 and this episode above. These are one of the twenty-eight-day restraining orders or the one-year non-molestation order.

They are supplementary stages in your route to freedom.

If the home is yours, you have the same choice. And if you opt for the non-molestation order, also go for the accompanying order within it to secure your home. In that way, you will make a fully legal claim to your home, whether you own it outright, have a mortgage or you live in rented accommodation. This is another stage.

3 When you reach the court stage, have all your documents to hand, even if, during Covid lockdowns or restrictions afterwards, the hearing may be virtual or by telephone.

4 This should be your final stage but, as events unfold over the next months, you have to make a personal decision to extend the non-molestation order after a year or to seek police protection if the respondent

infringes a court or police order in any way.

What my own case might have hinged upon but didn't was Elder Abuse.

What Is Elder Abuse?

The police and the courts concentrate on domestic abuse I suffered as a story of when things had gone wrong in a personal relationship.

Yet Elder Abuse was a cruel part of what happened.

Just as some young people are vulnerable to abuse in the home, so are some of their grandparents. The online proclamations of the domestic abuse commissioner mention that Age Concern tells us that elder abuse occurs when a person aged 65 or more suffers harmful physical, psychological, sexual, material or social effects caused by the behaviour of another person with whom they have a relationship implying trust.

Elder Abuse comes under 4 Categories

I adapted these next paragraphs from the webpage of the commissioner for domestic violence, not a character in my story but she may play an important role in your or your friends':

1 Physical Abuse: inflicting physical pain, injury or force.

2. Psychological Abuse: behaviour that causes mental or emotional anguish or fear.
3. Sexually abusive and exploitative actions entailing threats, force or the person's inability to give consent.
4. Financial Abuse: illegal or improper exploitation and, or, use of funds or other resources.

The commissioner expands her theme: "Elder intimidation is likely to feature yelling and threats of physical assaults, threats to leave or threats of suicide. The abuser also uses killer looks, physical actions such as pulling and shoving and hostile, daring expressions to instil fear. The abuser might also damage or destroy Items valuable to victims such as ornaments or important papers like bills and personal documents."

Well, you know this happened to me. Red did damage my pictures when he broke the glass or the frames besides some ornaments that I loved.

Mention of the commissioner begs this question:

What Good is the Commissioner for Domestic Violence?

Not how good but what good?

In 2019 the UK government appointed the aforesaid commissioner for domestic violence.

The domestic abuse commissioner tells us on her web page, "The Police make every effort to protect people from family violence, but they need to know it's happening."

I'm sorry to disabuse the righteous commissioner but this certainly wasn't my experience both before and since her appointment.

Along with doctors, police whose help I sought, ridiculed, denied me help and dismissed me not once or twice but over years.

Some of the commissioner's generalisations are telling, however.

1. For example, she asks why isn't domestic abuse reported as much as you might think? And the answer is standard and true:
   In many cases, the victim is too scared to speak out, fearing more violence. And that was certainly how I felt. This begs another question, in response to something we also know to be true.
2. In most cases, someone else knows domestic abuse is happening but does nothing about it. Why? This may be because they don't want to get involved or they don't want to be seen to be interfering.
   This was true of people who saw Red abusing me not physically but verbally and by crude behaviour in

pubs, at concerts and once most publicly in the Royal Albert Hall.

One person who caught Red attacking me physically used it not to get me help but to make a case to her mother for getting me out of their family home, which I was visiting.

The commissioner's home page has this dire warning: "The attitude that it's a private matter that should stay in the family no longer washes. Recent high-profile cases have shown that children, and adults, have died because no one reported the violence."

However, the commissioner's conclusion is simplistic:

"Stick up for the victims, and report any instance of family violence to the Police."

Simplistic, yes. Because it presumes consistent positive action by the police.

This aspect of domestic abuse when true friends get stymied in their attempt to help was a kernel of the plot about coercive control in the BBC soap *EastEnders* in 2021-22. Failed solicitor and serial killer Gray Atkins had already disposed of his first wife, Chantelle, then Tina the first person to guess that he had done so, and Kush a potential love rival. He killed Kush by pushing him to his death in the

Underground, crushed under an oncoming train.

Gray was then manipulating his second wife, once hard-as-nails and former drug mule Chelsea, so that she became a shadow of her former feisty self. And he managed to alienate her from Whitney and Kheerat, the true friends who understood the danger she was in so that she rejected them when she needed them most. There was a double whammy to this story since Chelsea's mother, core heroine Denise had also endured domestic abuse from her ex, religioso fanatic Lucas, culminating in weeks when Lucas held her prison in a cellar.

3   I think another reason why spectators are reluctant to intervene is that friends as well as doctors, social workers, etc., all too often find that, no matter how bad the behaviour, the victim will stay with the abuser because they can't think beyond their situation. Also, victims have a nagging sense that their abuser needs them emotionally and they still feel responsible for them. Hence, co-dependency. And so, given such a likely outcome to the scenario, police, doctors and social workers don't want to devote precious time and energy to help resolve a situation that the victim is not truly ready to leave. Further, the commissioner and other disability

experts proclaim that the police "are skilled at dealing with these situations, and will take appropriate action to protect victims."

This was far from my experience. My initial appeals for help from the police were met with contempt. And, even when I was on the path to a court order, one officer refused point-blank to help; two other officers couldn't distinguish between me as victim and Red as the abuser.

When police did make token offers of help, it was by barking orders at me, the victim, as if I was a bad dog.

Then there is this statement from the commissioner: "If you or anyone in your household is being abused or in any danger, don't hesitate to call 111. Police will respond quickly to help."

Have you tried to get help by dialling 111 only to find the phone rings and rings and rings without anyone answering?

***

Back to our story, mine and yours.

The second judge's confirmation of the non-molestation order was not the end of the affair between Red and me. There could be no fanfare salutes to the radiance of day as if I had escaped from a dark cave. The danger wasn't over.

As to Red, he was in his own private hell of imaginary bulging insects getting into his own bedroom in the doss house hotel, insects coming right through the cracks.

He sat up in the cheerless bedroom of the hotel as if the insects' feelers were scampering up and down his skin. Even when he brushed the non-existent insects away, their touch was still upon him. Crimson light from a police car stationed outside the hotel annexe shone through the tawdry hotel curtains. The light seemed to turn to blood as if the invisible nothings crawling everywhere had slashed an artery. Red recoiled as specks of blood splashed his hand and spread onto the white top sheet on the bed, staining it a lovely cerise that spread in shocking pink fingers. The stain moved of its own accord. It was like an octopus that lurched forward uneasily from the foot of the bed.

When Red turned and woke, he was sweating as never before.

***

Physically I was now safe. Or was it safer? No sooner had the second court hearing confirmed the non-molestation order than central government plunged the UK into its second full Covid-19 lockdown just before New Year 2021. It seemed like a prolongation of our city named Desire staying marooned as it was in Tier 4, except that, once again, so-called non-essential retail was brought to an abrupt end along with indoor places of recreation such as theatres and gyms, attending spectator sports outside and going inside to quaintly termed "hospitality" in cafes, restaurants and pubs.

Once again footfall in the city centre dwindled. Thus, it was safer for me to walk unchallenged until Spring 2021 when the government started to raise lockdown in stages.

As for Red, he was still going through a troubled time. In his gloom, he wrote to me again although this was forbidden by the court order. I was in a quandary. Although he had hurt me physically over the years, I didn't want him to suffer more emotionally or to feel he had nowhere he could call home.

His letter again reproached me for abandoning him.

"Please call me, Blue. I'm lonely. I need you to talk to me.

"Why have you done this to us? Please don't leave me on my own for summer this year like you did for my last birthday and Christmas."

But there was another plea:

"Hope you will send me something if you can. As I don't have much. You were my guardian angel. Love always, Red."

My neighbour, Jack, and another friend persuaded me I must report this letter to the police in case the letter became a pretext and prelude to more violence or systematic psychological undermining.

The police officer who came to answer my call for help was the brusque youngster who had already been to the flat several times. Red's letter encouraged him to assert a self-righteous tone. Red had broken the non-molestation order. Whoopee! And so Red had opened himself up for arrest and having to go to court.

Skimming Red's letter that he took from me, the sturdy policeman clearly saw this incident and his own ready response as kudos for him from his higher-ups, an easy victory since he knew Red's whereabouts. And, legally speaking, it was an open and shut case.

A little later that day, Red knew why the police had arrived to question him at the Milton Meadow Hotel. His last hope of reconciliation with me had gone. Pouf! When the police arrested and charged him, he was dumb not with fright but exasperation for this was denying him all hope.

"You are Red Hawk?" the officer asked in the hotel.

"Yes."

"Did you write a letter to Blue Sirocco four days ago?"

"Yes," Red mumbled, unsure where this unpleasantry was leading.

"You know you are subject to a non molestation order. It bars you from communicating with Blue Sirocco who is protected from you by a court order of last November."

"I meant no harm. I wanted Blue's help. I love him. He's all I have in the world."

"I'm arresting you for breaching the order. You know your rights."

Red crumbled in the back of the police car as it trundled its weary way to a distant station. He could hardly get his bearings in the station. The putty coloured walls blurred in his eyes as he tried – successfully - to hold back tears of desperation.

He was brought up sharp when a rotund sergeant - it must have been a sergeant - said, "We'll hold you here until the next court hearing. This is for your protection as well as Mr Sirocco's. We can't have you shooting off your mouth or going round to Mr. Sirocco's flat - I'm told you have a penchant for that - turning up unexpected and barging your way in. By holding you, everyone's protected - Mr. Sirocco, you and us."

"But I'm supposed to be back in my hostel by ten every night. If I'm not there, they'll throw me out."

"Let me see about that," said the desk sergeant. "Give me the name of your social worker. I'll call social services and let them know what's happened."

Red said nothing. He thought, "I have to keep my powder dry, play nicely nicely with them, just like I did with benefits officers."

Alone and bereft in his cell Red wasn't good at waiting but he knew it was necessary when he had to play submissive. What made it worse this time was that day turned into night three times before the hearing. His mind worked overtime:

"I want to scream till I kill someone with my voice, scream to keep me from climbing up these horrible walls, scream till I die.

"How could Blue do this to me, have me cooped up in a police cell? I've done nothing wrong. Just showed him that I love him and I want him back."

Yet and ironically, part of Red looked forward to what was inevitable: censure by the court. But now he was becoming more practical-minded, trying to concentrate on how he was going to get through the next few days.

When Red appeared at the court, there was a standby solicitor waiting for him there - Red didn't know the correct title or how it was this black woman was there to help him. She said sweetly,

"This court appearance seems far worse than it is. You plead guilty for breaching the court non-molestation order. If they ask you why, you explain that your mind is disturbed by all the calamities of the last few months - losing your home, your relationship and all this uncertainty about your future. The court won't be hard on you."

While Red and his solicitor were speaking in the lobby Red saw a worn white woman with bottle blonde hair whom he thought he knew. But he couldn't remember who she was or how he knew her.

Inside the court room the atmosphere was dry, the business perfunctory.

Red's solicitor advised the court, "My client is disabled, following a stroke. His ability to stand is further compromised by a serious injury to his leg and a painful operation to realign his knee and repair a torn ligament. This was after he was attacked on the street. This separate incident has nothing to do with the present case - except for the painful injury."

"But that didn't stop him repeatedly attacking his former partner who had cared for him."

This tart remark came from a waspish woman whom Red assumed was the chief judge or magistrate.

After some questions, answers and verbal sallies that Red couldn't hear, and addressing the little assembly, she pronounced verdict and sentence.

"Red Hawk, you are the respondent in a case leading to a non molestation order that prevents you from being in touch with, writing to or telephoning Mr Sirocco. Because of your recent serious injury and because, until this non mol order, you've never been in trouble, the sentence is six months--"

Red gasped.

"- suspended sentence and costs. The clerk tells me these are £175."

Red steadied himself on the rail at the front of the dock.

The clerk and your solicitor can discuss how you will pay."

The judge rose and left with a surly swish of her robes as they swept across her desk.

"Am I free to go?" Red asked the clerk.

"Yes, as soon you agree how you're going to pay court costs."

Red turned to his unsuccessful solicitor, who said,

"I've just heard about you getting an ESA award. It's likely that any back payment from ESA will cover the costs."

As they walked out of the court Red said to the solicitor. "It's unfair. I've only just got the award - rather been told about it. The money hasn't come through yet. Now this."

"The system gives you money with one hand and takes it away with the other," answered the solicitor.

"I'll say," said a harsh voice.

Red turned round. It was the bottle blonde he'd seen in the corridor. Now he remembered. She was the sister of Rusty who was married to Red's cousin, Chloe.

"I've got another message for you, boyo," she said with an expression somewhere between a smirk and a scold.

"Rusty and Chloe say, if you're thinking of getting back in touch with them, forget it. You dumped them years ago for your old man lover. Don't think of going there crying to them, now he's dumped you. From now on, you're on your own."

She thrust her little fat hand hand with its bitten nails upwards to wave Red away with a V sign.

***

Red knew fear all right, especially fear of the unknown. He felt his bowels stirring as if they were going to drop a heap of shit in his underpants, all casual-like. He knew he was too weak to make a half-decent attempt at a response in as public a place as a court. This court ruling and the bottle blonde's rejection seemed far worse than any minor brush with the law when he was a kid.

Then some relief came when the council assigned Red a new social worker who called on him. This was Genevieve Stiller, black-haired, bright and sparkling in manner. She had given up a behind-the-scenes career in showbiz when her young son, Gavin, was diagnosed with haemophilia. Then she learnt how much she and her family owed to local social services and the NHS. Becoming a social worker was her way of paying society back for helping preserve Gavin's fragile life.

"Are you alright?" she began to Red when they first met. "Let's see what we can do for you.

"And things *are* moving your way. I'm working on getting you a flat. Also, as you must have heard by now, I've been successful getting your ESA award increased to compensate for funds they took off you when Blue was looking after you. Now I'll have a go at getting your

PIP increased."

At that, Red fell in love with her a little, her shining black hair falling to the shoulders of her blue dress, ice blue in colour and dotted with daisies. She added, "But first, like I said, I'm going to find somewhere better, more suitable, for you to live." Then, unintentionally, Genevieve spoilt the rapport between them by asking, "So, now, are you alright?"

Instead of thanking her, Red sat on his hands and bit his tongue: "If she asks me just one more time if I'm alright, I'm gonna scream the house down. You wait and see if I don't. I really am going to scream until I die or she dies. Or something. Anything provided I don't cry."

***

When I heard later that in court Red had pleaded guilty and was given a suspended sentence, this was different from what I had imagined the scenario would be. The first judge had told me when he granted the non-molestation order, "If Red Hawk breaches the order, there's not much the police can do except tell him off."

I knew Red well enough to surmise how he would take things. All the sorts of things that heroes in TV and horror movies had battled with and won somehow in Red's life had got mixed up for worse, never for better.

With the court's inevitable process, it seemed that everything for good and bad over the last twenty years had dwindled into a massive disappointment. Yet Red refused to even contemplate the idea that any of it was his fault.

My social worker, Gladys, told me later, "Like many alcoholics, Red has convinced himself everything was someone else's fault."

"And that someone is me," I continued her unspoken thought.

She didn't reply to that. But she did add, "I have to congratulate you. You stood your ground. I thought you would give in."

"You mean take Red back? But the police were clear. Red was on a destructive path that could only end with my death. Apart from my feelings, I owe it to all of you, including the police, to stay true to the course you all set me on."

But upon Red's mis-conviction that it was all someone else's fault hinged another **smouldering problem**. As you know, the police had taken Red away from my flat in autumn 2020. His clothes and some other effects were still in my flat. Prompted by his friend Tom from the next town over, as I also said, I had cleaned and packed half of his clothes. Red had delayed taking them away the first time he had got back into my building. Then the police took the clothes away to their nearest station in part to eliminate another excuse Red might have for returning. Eventually, Red's new social worker Genevieve claimed them and ferried them back to him.

This left the other half of Red's clothes and shoes, his sofa, coffee table, various documents about DLA and PIP, electrical goods such as toaster, microwave, kettle, etc., and various hospital aids such as cane and Zimmer frame, all still in my flat.

The smaller items so dear to Red were his two favourite Man U coffee mugs, his teapot, his unread biography of his hero, Alex Ferguson, and his favourite opera, *Turandot*, in the recording with Joan Sutherland, Luciano Pavarotti and Montserrat Caballé. He had heard Caballé live once in a concert of opera excerpts at the Royal Albert Hall. Affectionately he called Caballé *Cabaret*. At that concert, when someone in the audience called out, "We love you," Montsy twirled her ample frame around and answered, "Truth."

Gladys, my social worker, had come as far back as December 2020 and surveyed Red's things, including various extra items such as crockery, cutlery and towels. She asked me to prepare an inventory, which I did.

"You're best to let Red have the electrical goods rather than paying him for them. However, we can provide him with such items when we have a secure flat ready for him. If you give up these items that you are using now, then we can present you with the same items that he doesn't need. Rather than returning the hospital items yourself, the correct procedure is to get them back to Red and for him to take them to the hospital. You cannot give him bedclothes. We do that."

In the light of what I had told the first judge, the court order provided for what was to happen to Red's effects. Since neither Red nor I could meet or communicate with one another, they were to go to him via an independent third party. This was to be the local council. And thereby hangs more of this lamentable tale.

Like I said, as early as the end of 2020 my social worker wanted to make sure everything was ready now, now, now:

"Don't hold me to it but I think Red will be in a council flat by the end of the month."

This was in December 2020.

That December, then January, February and March 2021 all passed without any confirmation or message. Each time I called social services for an update and further to have the council get Red's belongings back to him, social worker Gladys was unavailable. She did not return phone calls. Every two weeks I would again call the council switchboard who would put me through to social services. Each and every time a member of social services would listen patiently, take notes and send off an e-mail to Gladys or her manager.

I had thought I was being reasonable, even generous, in telling the court that Red had effects in my flat. But I got nowhere. I was left with cartons and bags of Red's belongings all this time, not to mention furniture and electrical goods.

I was in despair about anything being done. You might assume that the council would have a complaints office for citizens. Indeed, it did.

Those of you who work in offices will know how effective e-mails can be when your respondent doesn't want to bother, doesn't care, or is too embarrassed by their own failings to act. Pouf! In a flash the e-mail becomes invisible. It has disappeared. Eventually, I plucked up courage to complain and the switchboard operator put me through to Complaints.

I left a message.

The next day, the complaints officer, Jo, returned my call. I explained my situation.

"Red really does need his possessions, especially the

other half of his clothes and his DWP and PIP letters."

There followed a flurry of activity. This time social worker Gladys did call:

"Red has been shown a property in another suburb and he's accepted it. His new social worker, Genevieve, arranged this. There's a support worker on hand at the property to help Red. However, I'm asking if, to help us, you would wait for another week before we move his belongings. Red is too overwhelmed with managing his new flat to be able to take delivery of his effects."

A week later social services claimed they had no funds to transport clients' belongings and no storage facilities for them either.

***

Why Am I Telling You All This?

I appreciate that this rigmarole may test your attention beyond reasonable limits. But if you are a victim struggling to break free, then this is the sort of argumentative quagmire you may have to go through when you divest yourself of your abuser but they still have rights to their possessions.

ADVICE

When you finally get the law on your side, it is essential

that the break is complete. Try and arrange for your abuser's possessions, clothes and anything else to get to them as soon as possible. Otherwise, your inner pain will go on and on.

***

In my case, after yet another week, the council's excuse for more inaction was that Red refused to accept his things. His social worker, Genevieve Stiller, would try him again over the next two weeks.

I pointed out,

"Surely, Red needs the other half of his clothes and shoes. His box of DWP, DLA, PIP and bank letters is important for him. And the hospital Zimmer frame, metal crutch and Islam prayer mat belong to the hospitals. You could have sent them back six months ago."

And again, "Surely he wants the rest of his clothes?"

"No. Nothing. That's Red's decision," said Genevieve. "And he's of sound mind."

I argued back.

"But his clothes would be expensive to replace. If he can't see sense about this, doesn't that throw into doubt that he is of sound mind?"

Red's social worker didn't want to answer that one.

"Unfortunately. Red won't listen to any practical suggestions."

"So, I've kept everything here for seven months all for nothing, except my own inconvenience."

"The items could go to a charity for women who are victims of domestic abuse."

"OK. You've corralled me into this but OK. However, for my legal protection, I ask you for an official letter authorising my retaining and, or, dispersing Red's effects."

We went round and round the mulberry bush about this. The two social workers suggested to Red that, if he did not want his effects, then he might sign a letter releasing them. This, of course, he would not do.

My offstage friend, Ben, said, "Typical. Red will always do anything to be contrary. And in this case, to be spiteful."

Given Red's contrariness, my social worker's next suggestion was:

"Genevieve and I have discussed this. We suggest you should serve a notice on Red and us that you retain everything for another full month and, if they are not collected after that, you can either retain or dispose of Red's possessions."

"I think what you're not telling me is that, although

the mess is partly caused by social services, social services will not provide me with an official letter authorising me to dispose of everything in case there are legal implications that might come back to bite you. And after so long, why do I have to wait another month?"

"That's because with a notice like this you have to give sufficient time for the respondent to take stock and to make arrangements. And I think it best if you construct four separate notices, separating Red's possessions into four separate categories: shoes and clothes; electrical and household goods; documents; furniture, the large sofa and glass coffee table. This will allow Red to choose if he wants some types of items and not others.

"If you could send me an e-mail stipulating all this, my department can print it out and I will bring it to you for signature the day after tomorrow. Then Genevieve can serve the four notices on Red."

So, thus pressurised, this is what we did.

Here is one of the letters I wrote:

"Notice on Red Hawk Property

"Over the past seven months, I have looked after items of Red Hawk in the hope that he could arrange for them to be collected by the city council and delivered to him at a secure address. This hasn't happened. According to the court order of 2020, any collection has to be through a third party.

"I now give notice that, if the following items are not collected by Thursday 30 June 2021, I shall, in consultation with the two social workers, retain or dispose of them as seems most appropriate.

"Plastic Box containing:

"Red's business correspondence, bank letters, letters from DWP, DLA and PIP correspondence

"Biography of Alex Ferguson

"Miscellaneous medication

"Please note: the official correspondence provides information that may prove important for Red's benefit applications later; the DLA letters might be irreplaceable.

"Signed: Blue Sirocco."

At long last Red did see sense, not only about his clothes but also about almost everything else. He also demanded a small Clas Ohlsson music centre that we had shared in my flat. For the sake of harmony in an exasperating scenario, I gave in to Red's demand and carefully packed everything up, cushioned by bubble wrap.

Genevieve, Red's social worker, came with one of her superiors to carry almost everything off to Red in the superior's station wagon.

What was left were the sofa, coffee table, hospital aids and the music centre.

Three weeks later Genevieve Stiller phoned to ask me if she could come over that afternoon. She arrived bearing a cleaned and repaired puce coloured plastic kitchen bin.

"I'm returning it because it has your papers at the bottom; also, this black jacket and white shirt, both suitable for funerals. Red says they're yours. Red has signed over the sofa and the coffee table for you. They're too big for his new apartment. He's changed his mind about the hi-fi, as well. He doesn't want it."

"But last time you were here, you said he demanded it. I've packed it very carefully. I bought a small replacement for myself."

"He's changed his mind. That is that."

With that, Genevieve collected the remaining hospital aids. There wasn't even a whisper about the repeated previous suggestion of sending the unwanted belongings to a battered wives' charity.

Then, clearly immersed in what she saw as a mini tragedy in her personal affairs that had nothing to do with Red or me, she said,

"I'm mourning my own partner's political problems with his appointment in Religious Studies at a university nearby."

She said, "He's been canned, denied renewal of his contract. The department has had to face cuts and my partner is a casualty. He's in Religious Studies. This is an irreligious age. My partner doesn't know where to turn. We expected more of his department, integrity."

She was more than a little surprised that I could put my finger on the small-mindedness of university politics of which her partner was apparently now a lost victim.

"Integrity?" I repeated her word.

"That's an expensive word," I continued. "You see, at universities the professors and lecturers are highly trained in specific areas, pleasing themselves. Once they're established, ensconced in a university post, their days of ardour and striving are over. They get their teaching and administration off tap. But their over-active, imaginative minds are free to roam. This is not for the better. They reserve the better part of themselves, their scholarship, for any papers they may care to write. And instead of their day-to-day dealings being of the highest order for the betterment of mankind, their party politics, one-upmanship, and self-conceit take over. They have all this time on their hands and self-interest consumes them.

"It comes as a shock to us outsiders. Not that we've not experienced office politics and gamesmanship in our own different careers. We certainly have. But we expect more of university professors, better use of their creative juices and energy. And that's not forthcoming."

"How do you know all this? It's as if you were a fly on the wall in my partner's department."

I shrugged winsomely.

"I'm just glad you didn't say I was a wasp buzzing around in a cake shop."

I was off on one of my tangents:

"Composer Vaughn Williams wrote music for a Cambridge production of *The Wasps* by Aristophanes. I think it's about quarrelling, spiteful people. Late comedy writer Barry Cryer told a joke about a man who went into a cake shop, asking, 'Do you sell wasps?'

"'The shop owner said, "This is a cake shop. Of course, we don't sell wasps.'

"'But you've got a wasp in the window.'"

And social worker Genevieve left that day, probably thinking I was a good egg, albeit an eccentric one. She didn't suspect I was poking fun at her and the other social workers who had ignored, disregarded and poked fun at me like so many buzzing wasps who would sting any of you, dear readers, without any compunction.

***

As coronavirus infection rates fell in summer 2021, whatever the variations of the virus, the government began to ease Covid restrictions.

Once bars opened first outdoors, then indoors as well with elaborate use of plastic sheeting as a gesture to social distancing, Jack Rascal suggested, "I think we should try one pub out, ready to outstare any friends of Red who may be ready to threaten you."

So, one fine afternoon we went to the Glass House. Jack was all emphatic purpose; inside I was timorous. I had steeled myself in advance. A habitual soak sitting in the next plastic booth accosted me. He was unmerciful:

"Whatever filthy kind of life you still have is all wrapped up in your new loser lover," he said, meaning Jack. Jack missed this because he was distracted by a commotion farther along the bar. And we weren't lovers.

"You know it and Jack knows it," continued the pesky soak. "He planned to use you from the very beginning, except that *planned* is the wrong word since you thought you were acting impulsively, independently. Your new slag will take you for every last penny you've got. And Jack is as shit-faced as you. You're just made for one another. Simple. You deserve one another. He won't keep you for long. You don't bother Red, the pair of you, one fucking bit. As I told him, Red's well out of it."

ADVICE
5 Harsh Lessons

1. To repeat myself – it's my only fault – and to underline the point:

   Among the chief difficulties, and one that is supreme for anyone escaping an abuser is that the escape has to be permanent, no matter what residual feelings you have for the person who has attacked you. Your escape has to be all or nothing. That's so easy to say. But when there are children involved or common property, mere physical escape is not the end of your problems.

2. But next comes another, more frightening decision. What is to happen to the abuser, your abuser? A criminal trial and possible prison sentence? Their being cast adrift and made homeless? If either you (the victim) or your abuser have families to turn to, they may provide the answer in the short run. Rarely in the long run of "forever homes," as pet rescue TV

programs put it. But if you as a victim don't have a thought-through Plan B for what happens after you divest yourself of your abuser, then it's likely your dilemma will flag up an almighty red sign to stop you in your tracks. For you are coming to the emotionally fraught roadblock of all or nothing.

3 You must seal yourself off from contact with your abuser. You must cast him or her out. He or she must be banned forever. Here the official line of courts is correct. For any contact, even expressed as regret by your abuser can only lead to more trouble for you, whether it will compromise you in the eyes of the law or lead to renewed violence or psychological threats. Thus, the break when it comes, or when you achieve it, has to lead to unbridgeable separation.

4 And unless the physical abuse you've put up with was so gross as to endanger your very life, then facing up to enforced legal separation for both parties can seem psychologically disturbing. But you have to face it.

5 Separation by non-molestation order is like a death warrant and, like death, it's best if it happens quickly. But in my case, Red's uncontrollable anger and confusion were even worse than killing him. It was

degrading him. Drink was stealing his youth before he was even middle-aged. And this frightened him.

What Next?

Once you've escaped from your abuser and feel safe enough to take stock of your new situation, you will still need help but from whom?

I was once in a seminar organised by the city of Desire to help people who had lost their jobs to find work. The moderator encouraged us all to use, to utilise, our contacts in order to cast as wide and deep a net as possible in our search for work.

One troubled man asked the moderator, "How far dare we go in getting help from friends, family or people in work?

"How much pressure can we put on friends to get a job? When is too much too much?"

The answer was logical and blunt.

"Go on asking until they tell you to stop."

And the same answer applies to any of you who not only need help to escape your abuser but also help to start your lives all over, and that means living, resettling and maybe getting work or benefits so that you have enough to live on.

If you have been abused, this is not the time for

social niceties. Your life and well-being are more important than anything else or anyone else's interests or feelings.

At the worst of my unfolding crisis with Red, I had Ben, a dear friend who lived on the far edge of the city, and who would have let me stay in his spare bedroom. The outsize handicap was that he lived miles from any bus stop and miles from his local railway station. And going there would have handed me another outsize problem: I would have left my flat. If you live in any town centre you will know that anyone up to no good can get into your building by hook or by crook. And when they can do that and they are equally determined, they can break into your flat. You may have superior legal rights but, if someone breaks into your property, the damage has been done.

So, in my troubled case, I had to stay in my flat to maintain my property rights. And this put me at personal risk of being attacked by Red or his friends. This is why the court non-molestation order was essential for my safety as well as my peace of mind. And it did not come easily or quickly.

EPISODE 7

Everlasting Ache

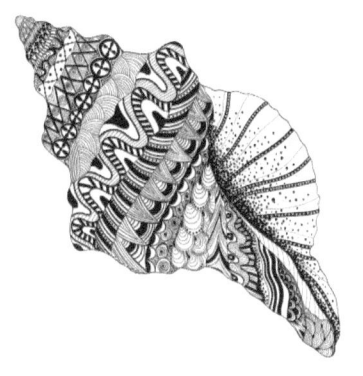

Urinetown is the title of an American musical of 2001. And I'm sorry to tell you it might as well have been the name of the mess I was in at the end of my story, first being urinated upon metaphorically by an unjust judge, then by Red Hawk physically in the lobby outside my flat.

As autumn 2021 drew nearer I dreaded having to apply to the Family Court for an extension of the non-molestation order for another twelve months. And with good reason did I dread it. My inner sense told me that the progress of my request would prove as tortuous the second time around in 2021 as the original application in 2020. Events proved me right.

I gave myself a month before the original order expired to have everything ready for the court.

The first problem was that I didn't know the exact number or code of the extension application form.

"We're not allowed to tell you," said the young woman's voice on the phone when I asked the court applications team. "That would count as giving you legal advice. And we're not allowed to do that."

It seemed to me that if you are an applicant and simply know you require a form to have your non-molestation order extended, that should be enough for a court to send you the form and tell you how it is termed, if differently, inside the court. But no.

The Law Society suggested three solicitors who might tell me the code number of the right form. I took the names of three solicitors. As had happened in 2020 when the solicitors named by the Law Society in London had all proved duds, it was the same with this new list in 2021. Either the solicitors didn't exist locally or wouldn't help because my need was not their speciality. Nevertheless, scrutinising the web – as best I could - did provide names and contact details of solicitors who, for a tiny fee, would offer advice through their websites. For £5 I learned that the form I required was FL 403.

Thus prompted, I asked the court application office for FL 403. The same court worker who had declined to help me earlier sent me the form. In one important particular she gave extra help. Learning that I was visually impaired and would have difficulty scanning any document and sending it via e-mail to Slough (as had gone wrong so spectacularly in 2020), she asked her supervisor who agreed I could submit the application on paper through the regular post to the court.

Form FL 403 is way shorter than the form for the original non-molestation order. But as with so many government forms, it does not allow enough space for certain answers.

My experiences the previous year had taught me something of what to expect from the court's circumlocution processes but perhaps not enough fear about things going wrong.

I had prepared my statement in support of my extension request in advance, concentrating on Red's unfortunate letter in breach of the original order and the tangled struggle to get his possessions back to him, something that had further soured relations between us.

If I wanted to conceal my address, telephone number or any other details I had to leave them blank on form FL 403 and add them to a separate form C8. So, I had to phone the applications team again and ask for this second form and add it to the first. Where I thought sections needed utmost clarity such as Red's addresses via his new social worker, I typed these portions, printed them courtesy of the PC room in the town library and pasted them onto form FL 403.

This would not do for the court officials who insisted I scanned them into the form and then returned them through the internet.

All that was at stake in Form C8 was my new telephone number meant to be kept from Red.

This problem of my not being able to scan

information resulted in the court returning the forms to me yet again and this caused further delay.

More trouble came with the difference between my interpretation of the instructions about what was to be concealed and how it was to be concealed.

What I needed to keep from Red was not my local address and e-mail address that Red knew because he had lived there but my new phone number.

This seemed clear enough to me. But when a court secretary read the order back to me on the phone, she failed to read the final bracketed instruction, thereby changing the meaning to the court's new interpretation.

When I asked for help, the manager was brusque enough to start barking at me, "Fill in your name, then your phone number, and sign and date the document. Nothing else."

For the sake of at least getting my request to a judge in a timely fashion, I gave in to the court's interpretation.

Time was short. If the court could not have the FL 403 request by the final day of the original non-molestation order, that non-molestation order would expire on its designated day at 4.00 pm and I would have to start the entire process again, applying for a new non-molestation order.

However, with all the to-ing and fro-ing, not to mention delays in the internal process of any document getting to the right department inside the court building, although I had started the process a month ahead of the final date covered by the non-molestation order it was now only five days before the expiration date that the court had a document presented in a way that satisfied the court secretariat.

I guess that from their point of view the court secretariat thought they had bent over backwards metaphorically speaking, to accommodate my sensory problems by allowing me a paper application in the first place and then explaining everything so carefully.

3 Pieces of Constructive Advice to the Family Court

1 The court should have available, ready on their computers and ready to print, forms in large print for VIPs, and not simply a standard small print size on the assumption that one design fits all VIP categories. Apart from forms in Braille, VIPs who have some sight usually ask for large print in bold on sans serif font on yellow or cream paper.

2 Compose court instructions so that they mean what the court intends and not something else.

And if, as part of the court secretariat, you are

reading forms out to a VIP, get the words complete and get the sense right.
3 When the court secretariat sends out orders for court hearings it should get the day, time and location right.

***

You see, the next problem was that the court order for me to attend the hearing was incorrect, precisely stipulating an appearance at the court which was false since the hearing was to be by MS Teams, something I didn't understand and couldn't access.

After yet another telephone discussion the court decided that the hearing was to be by phone and before a so-termed floating judge.

***

In answer to the lead question on the extension application form implied by, "Your reasons for applying," I wrote:

"I live in anxiety and fear. In 2020 I argued for the original non-molestation order on grounds of habitual physical violence, especially when Red Hawk was drunk, as well as psychological abuse and mental cruelty when he was sober.

"Despite standard restrictions imposed on him by

the original non-molestation order, Red Hawk has tried to get around the order, to confront me and inveigle me into supporting him.

"In spring 2021 he wrote a letter, part reproving, part cajoling, part accusing me of abandoning him to nothing, and asking me to be in touch at his (then) address. I told the police (as they had ordered me to do). A police officer called at my flat, took the letter away and arrested Red, who later pleaded guilty in court.

"And there has been the almighty mess of the council delaying and delaying restoring his clothes and other effects to him."

However, there was to be no happy ending. My spoiler alert for you, my readers, is that when the hearing by phone took place, the judge ruled against me.

At the time of the hearing, I could not give the judge's name. I still cannot give you the judge's name. The herald who announced the call mumbled the judge's name and so did the judge. To me, he was and remains Humbug 2021.

The non-identified judge told four untruths in his summary dismissal at the hearing.

1st Untruth:

"I've read all the papers," he began.

It became clear during the hearing that he had not.

"I deny your application for an extension."

2nd Untruth:

"You've done nothing about the case for a year."

I had alerted both police and social services to problems across the year as they happened.

3rd Untruth:

"And suddenly you've alerted the court only five days before the original order is about to expire. Then you've designated the matter as *urgent*."

I had not. The court secretariat had labelled the case as urgent and without telling me. So, the unnamed humbug judge was finding me a chancer who was undeservedly playing the system.

The judge concluded, "The original non-molestation order ends at 4.30 pm on Friday and that is that. I am depriving you of police protection after that. There is no system of appeal in a case like this." Yes, you've spotted it. The judge also got the time wrong.

Was the unjust judge unaware that the most dangerous time for victim escapees from domestic abuse is once they are clearly and cleanly away from their abusers?

All I was allowed to say was, "I applied for the extension a month ago in October."

I could hear the unjust judge rummaging in the

papers.

"Is this letter of 25 October with your summary, part of your application?"

"Yes."

"Even so my decision stands. I will amend my notes."

"Will the court send me notification of your denial?"

"Yes. I see you are partially sighted."

"I'm on the blind register."

"I see. How would you like the official letter to be presented? In 24 point?"

"No, 14 or 16-point in a sans serif font in bold."

4th Untruth:

"Then that is the way the notice will come to you."

***

You will understand that I was devastated by all this, the judge's adverse ruling, his harsh characterisation of me, and the likelier prospect of more trouble ahead. The judge had accused me of playing the system when I had been responsible and accurate.

I am a UK citizen and resident in the UK. I am also poor, old and disabled. I have a right to seek help from the police on serious matters of crime and personal safety.

Only one of his missteps was the judge willing to partially correct: moving the date of my application from November to October 2021.

The court herald proclaimed that the court hearing was discreet, in-camera, and I must not divulge what was said outside the hearing. If this is true, it seems unjust.

My only way to protest was to write a letter of complaint to the Justice Secretary - not to have the judgement overruled but to show a miscarriage of justice even if the Ministry of Justice took no action.

I phoned the Ministry of Justice to clarify the subject and form of the letter, to whom it should be addressed and how, as well as the ministry address in Petty France in London. The court man I spoke to said, "A letter like this has to go to the secretary of justice and written on paper and sent through regular post."

"How long will it be before I receive acknowledgement or reply?"

"About six weeks. If you do not hear from the ministry by then, call us back."

I knew I couldn't appeal the adverse decision. And I didn't think any protest I could make would receive a sympathetic hearing. But I felt keenly that I had been treated unjustly and that the Ministry of Justice should hear a complaint, have to acknowledge it, hopefully keep it in its files, and, whatever the resistance of the staff, emerge better informed and enlightened and perhaps to acknowledge it.

Fat chance.

It turned out that everything the ministry official had told me was wrong apart from the address.

2 Problems of Access at the Ministry of Justice

1 In my letter, I told the justice secretary, "What is clear is that the judge and the secretariat are in serious want of disability awareness training. Disabled people's needs are not limited to such important mechanical aspects as the right sort of print formats and access for wheelchair users. It extends to ensuring the safety needs of disabled people who may need extra protection from harm, psychological as well as physical.

"Although he did not swear and curse, the judge's whole manner was that of a pompous bully, self-satisfied as he denied me an extension.

"I cannot challenge the judge's decision ruling. It stands as a declaration of legal hostility to one disabled person. I await my fate even if this means more sporadic violence against me.

"I am entitled to my opinion that the judge is

demonstrably below professional standard."
2. Finally, "And I ask you, with help from local disability groups across the country, to devise and implement disability awareness training course for judges and court secretariat. Recall that disabled people of working age (like yourself) comprise 20 per cent of their age cohort, and higher, perhaps to 24 per cent in the Northwest."

***

In the meantime, I was left with the obstinate fact that the unjust judge had ruled.

In my story of surviving domestic abuse, I had moved from darkness to light and had now been thrust back again into darkness. I was to be left alone with my problem.

A day or so after the judge's ruling, I got Red's response, his rejoinder.

One morning I noticed a really bad smell in the little lobby on my floor just outside the lift. The smell was so bad, so pungent, I thought it was excrement. And, given the sorry history of mis-plumbing in our converted building, I assumed there was a leak from a soil pipe somewhere. But when the young cleaner of the building was vacuuming our lobby floor later that day, I asked if she could smell the same smell that I did.

"Oh yes," she said. "It's wee."

I had no doubt who had done it. Red knew how to get into the building and how to use the lift. And, as I've already told you, he certainly knew how to piss somewhere inconvenient. The smell was rank. But I had no proof. And by now with furtive attempts at cleaning, the site had been compromised. I couldn't request a police investigation.

But I believed Red had left his mark, urinated like a skilled mammal to leave his indelible scent where it would matter most to me and as a warning of what might come later. So, the end of this book heralds the beginning of an uncertain future.

3 Shortcomings at the Ministry of Justice in Dealing with Citizen's Concerns

1 The officers at my local Carers Forum wanted to hear about my case. One of these officers explained she was also a JP and that I should have sent in my complaint to the ministry on an online form.

This advice was also problematic in several respects. Yes, I learned when I phoned the ministry to find out what had happened to my original letter, that the ministry was not accepting any paper submissions because of Covid so it was wrong of anyone on the ministry's secretariat during Covid-19 to have advised me differently.

2. Then the requisite MoJ form specifically excludes complaints about judges. That very proscription speaks volumes. It suggests that prospective complaints about judges are common.

Then, of course, for a disabled person on the blind register even with a scintilla of residual sight, the ministry application form has problems. An impossible hurdle for a VIP accompanied by contradictory advice from call handlers, the first people you are likely to speak to when you phone in with a concern. On the phone, trying to find out the correct way to write to the MoJ, I was given various pieces of information all at odds with one another.

I was told to find a website labelled JCIL. This led to more contradictory sites such as *Jesus Christ is Living* and *Journals of Islamic Studies*. Then I was told to go to JCIO.

3. In short, the whole apparatus of the ministry dedicated to responding to the public seems designed as a scaffold to prevent, to forestall, legitimate complaints and provide the ministry with a mechanism to ignore, deny, deride and cancel

complaints.

By now, of course, the focus of my complaint had widened so what was at stake was not simply an errant judge but the ministry itself.

Three months after my original letter to the Ministry of Justice I received a reply to that very letter that the MoJ website explicitly declared would not be answered if it was sent my regular Post Office mail.

This MoJ letter ordered me as to where I should go with links to various websites – again all impossible for me, a VIP, to negotiate. It was a classic instance of disability evasion based on the discredited medical model of disability.

In my reply, I thanked the civil servant for his or her courteous reply to my original letter - "courteous except for the sentence where you are openly rude."

While the MoJ reply was at pains to advertise the probity of the ministry, the details in the letter told a different story.

Although the original non molestation case explained that I was on the blind register - and that my preferred accessible presentation was a sans serif font in 14 or 16 point size in bold - the MoJ worker wrote back in miniscule font.

The letter proudly proclaimed that judges received

specific training in disability issues.

In my reply, I answered back, "If this does take place, it is obviously ineffective."

Furthermore, "From my experience with two court cases, the Family Court seems to have no standby provision for presenting material to visually impaired applicants. And the unjust judge of November 2021 - if he was not being malicious - simply hasn't a clue about the psychological aspects of disability prejudice."

Taken as a whole and from my perspective the MoJ defence was what some might term the bug letter - a standard dismissive reply of a restaurant to a patron who has been served an unwanted, unpalatable insect along with his meal.

5 Hard Won Pieces of Advice to the Ministry of Justice

1 Worse, the indefensible advice came courtesy of an unfortunate hoity toity tone. The civil servant told me I needed to, had to, write to, to speak to, or whatever to whoever he or she ordered me.

But I was not their employee nor did I report to them. There was no point in advising someone like me who doesn't see properly to look up links on a website. Nor should any government department expect that a friend or a family member should undertake this.

2. Ban the phrase "People with disabilities."

   The giveaway that the ministry had got solidified in, glued by, and stuck in formaldehyde came with the outdated and discredited phrase "people with disabilities." This phrase reeks of the discredited medical model of disability. If civil servants in the ministry use such terms and genuinely don't understand what is wrong with them, then that is another nail in the coffin of the MoJ's touted validation of disabled people's rights and government duty of care.

3. When responding to the public, take control of your logistics. Get your facts, your directions, your reactions in a logical order.

   The irony was that the civil servant was replying to my original letter to the secretary when, after waiting six weeks for a reply, someone else at the MoJ had told me that I should not have written to the chief lawyer in the first place. Rather I should have filled in a complaints form on a difficult website. I did so and still await some form of reply concentrating on MoJ inadequacies to disabled people.

4 If there is a leader, a secretary, a manager, a minister allegedly in charge, he or she should take responsibility for what happens, what goes wrong, in his department.

I hadn't expected the minister himself to write back to my first letter. His response or lack of it was exactly what I would expect of someone who denied cavorting on a beach while Afghanistan fell.

I wrote to him because this was what I was first told to do.

5 What none of us expects from a Ministry of Justice is that it facilitates crime. And any argument that the MoJ does not know what it is doing or has done is hardly a defence.

In a constructive spirit I urged MoJ civil servants to commission and attend disability awareness training classes.

***

During the height of my terror with Red I felt a sort of suffused fear. I was able to move because I had things to do, to run the home, etc., but the cumulative effects of the pandemic, the degradation I had experienced at the hands of the third judge, and the stonewall of silence from the Ministry of Justice had replaced the old fear of physical violence. Now I felt lethargy caused by the hopelessness of my situation, by being denied police protection and weighed down by establishment indifference.

A fourth shortcoming of the way the Ministry of Justice handles the endemic problem of domestic abuse deserves an entire section to itself. And this is when a case of domestic abuse breaks undoubted criminal boundaries and where what amounts to an unofficial Statute of Limitations, brings a guillotine down on police intervention and court action. It deserves a subsection of its own:

Time Limit in Court Cases

A BBC text on Friday 15 October 2021 told us that there was a huge rise in domestic abuse cases being dropped by police, so they were never getting to court:

"Victims of domestic abuse are seeing their cases dropped at an increasing rate, according to data obtained by the BBC. Police have six months to charge common assault cases, including domestic abuse, from when the alleged incident took place.

"Campaigners say this is unfair because of the complex nature of many cases. Figures show 3,763 cases were dropped for this reason in the past year [2021] compared with 1,451 cases four years earlier."

So, there was a time limit of six months from the alleged assault for cases to be pursued in court. It was, as I say, in effect, a statute of limitations. as incisive and cruel as any parliamentary guillotine.

Thus, continued the BBC text, "13,000 cases were dropped over five years. Campaigners say women are being denied justice and police and prosecutors should be given extra time."

Belatedly the government started to consider redress for the problem of abuse cases falling down before they even got to court. In autumn 2021 the then home secretary announced proposals to extend what I term the statute of limitations in domestic abuse cases from six months to two years. Reformers considered this extension also too little.

None of us chose the times or the circumstances we have been born into. But we should make the most of them and our own lives. And try to make a better world for all of us. And "we" should include the MoJ.

***

In my story, in my own home, I was disturbed by nightmares. I dreamed everything in unearthly slow motion.

One night I awoke to creaky noises in the lobby outside the flat. As a long-time flat dweller, I'm used to hearing people coming and going at all sorts of times, day and night. Slight noise doesn't bother me. But the creaks that night, either in a bad dream or when I had just woken, were different. There was banging on the security partition door between the lift and the lobby on my floor. It was quite distinct: the noise of someone who didn't know the security code to open the inner door or who couldn't make the code work and was desperate to get through that security door. The only person I knew of who had ever come in and shouldn't have been there was Red Hawk.

Somebody rang my doorbell. The sound pierced the night. I sat bolt upright in bed. This was not a bell downstairs and outside the building but just outside my individual front door. This was where the Contact Centre men of social services who fitted enabling devices for disabled people had placed a doorbell with amplified sound. In the middle of the night, it could sure awaken the dead.

On that disturbed night when I turned around still halfway between dream and reality, I saw Red staggering towards me down my hall, his face with doughy running flesh, his eyes black like tarmacadam on the roads. He boasted, "I beat you because I wanted to fuck you, Blue, that's all I wanted."

A new voice spoke inside my mind. It was a jocular, squealing voice. I had a numbing certainty that it was Red inside my head or on some crazy internal radio, a wireless for the blind gone rogue.

"Outside, things look larger than they really are, don't you think?" Red cooed from somewhere inside my head.

"Go away," I stammered.

Silence. Red had gone. Or had he?

My gut feeling was that this was a stinking, rotten flat where everything was wrong, the doors, the windows, the heating and, above all, the plumbing. And if it wasn't wrong yet, it was wrong a moment later.

"The house that Jack built," Red used to call it when he lived there. When I put on the bedside light, the angles of the corners were wrong. The perspective was in flux, undulating, like girls' dresses when they danced to disco. The bedroom ceiling seemed to rise higher and higher and then came crashing down. It wasn't real. Or was it my twisted eyesight?

Red must be outside in the hallway, come to get me. The lumpy mattress underneath me began to wobble as if it, too, were dancing to a disco beat.

I heard a buzzing in the hall.

Was I going mad?

Fearfully, I got up to investigate.

I stepped onto the laminate floor and would have skidded across it but I had the computer desk to hold on to. When I switched on a second light, the room snapped back to its accustomed shape and size like being released back by an elastic band. When I jerked my front door open, its hinges squeaked like a dull scream. Then everything went silent like a tomb.

When I opened the security door between our inner lobby and the lobby to the elevator, the different hallway light made everything glow orange.

Red spoke again.

"Your flabby old face is screwed up like terror on steroids. And you've got much to be frightened of, like you frightened me, scared me to death with your invasion of body snatchers, aka the men in blue, the bluebottle cops. Now it's your turn to feel the power of fear: uncontrollable fear, pure and simple."

Of course, I didn't know if Red really was in the building. I genuinely thought he was, which was why I phoned Jack Rascal who was still awake bingeing on muscle fantasy movies. But when he arrived in my building ten minutes later, he found no shape to match the creaking noise I had described. I was frightened sure enough and perhaps being silly. The fact that Jack had walked up and down the six stories, all 120 steps, to check if someone really was there and finding nobody didn't allay my fears. Yes, I was nervous. My battle for security was paramount far too much of the time.

Before he asked, I gave Jack £20, which was all the money I had. When Jack left, somewhat disgruntled, and I was alone with my thoughts I could see Red's face as large as life hovering above the foot of my bed. I knew it was only a frightful illusion but one detail struck me. Red's eyes seemed to get larger, to grow. The flecks of dark grey in their icy irises flickered like clouds scurrying before a storm. Red was livid with me. I knew that. But his expression was tinged with helplessness as if he were staring at me from a bottomless pit. His expression was a mix of hate and pain. He wasn't finished yet. He spoke,

"I'm gonna eat you up, what's left of you unless you give me back my life and my inheritance. I huffed and I puffed and I told that useless social worker Reza and the cringing replacement Genevieve straight exactly what I think about you and your airs.

"She got me more ESA and some PIP sure enough. Then she didn't want to know. She fucked me off, just like everyone else does."

Red's hateful words from our horrible Christmas Day with CR came back loud and clear to haunt me,

"You think this is just a bad dream and you're going to wake up. That's right. Well, let me tell you this, Blue Belle or whatever the fuck you call yourself these days: When you do wake up, you're going to wake up in hell, the hell of your own guilty conscience."

And with that, Red's lopsided grin became a murderer's grimace. When he opened his mouth, instead of his teeth broken by cocaine, they showed plastic gums, disfiguringly crimson.

Then his mood changed. Red's bleary smile turned into a leer. He winked an eye, like cocking a snook, as if to say, "See ya in the morning, bright as a button."

I felt Red was still inside me, that he would never go away.

But it wasn't just Red who could kick me in the teeth. So could the court.

***

I waited in vain for a court letter or e-mail confirming and detailing the unjust judge's pronouncement. I waited for one, two, three months. Then four and five months passed without any official transcript, summary or e-mail.

It was during this period that the not-so mysterious urine spray spread itself outside my flat. And it was also during this time that I was in touch with the Ministry of Justice, three times by phone and three times by letter or e-mail. And suddenly, hey presto! the family court sent me the peremptory dismissal of my application for a non molestation extension, five-and-a-half months after the court hearing.

The court e-mail held 4 surprises for me

1. At last I learnt the judge's name (which I cannot reveal to you). Was this his real name, a pen name (such as I have for this book), or what?
2. The judge swept aside - ignored - his comments at the hearing implying I had been first over-tardy about getting my appeal to the court and then over-hasty in demanding urgent court attention. Instead of his accusation that I had played the system in a high-and-mighty fashion, he now said I was excused blame over problems in getting my application to court.
3. And most important – even worse of all - he trumpeted a new reason for dismissing my application. I now learnt that I was not in danger from Red Hawk, that I had not produced any evidence to suggest that I was and I hadn't signed

any affidavit as to the truth of my statement.

I hadn't been told by anyone in the court secretariat that such a declaration was part of the application process. There was no word about this either in the form or any spoken instructions. And the judge had said nothing of the sort in the hearing.

Whatever he now wrote in the document, was he being disingenuous, politically sidestepping his unfortunate remarks, or what?

4 There was no explanation, no apology for the inordinate delay in the court writing to me. Was it simply that the court had to deal with such a backlog of all sorts that it took almost six months to publish its rulings on me? I wondered if the court might have been alerted in some way that I had been in touch with the Ministry of Justice and that had perhaps prompted some retrospective action. Was it another example of the ways in which the UK is becoming like a third world country if measured by its sluggish rate of efficiency?

ADVICE

In my final advice section, I let my mind wander and then rein in my conclusions ever tighter.

1 The institution of the court doesn't do itself any favours in a letter pretending that November in one year is today in the following May.
2 And a judge does himself no favours by declaring that his reasons for dismissing an application is based on something that he never mentioned, never asked about, at the hearing – namely that I was in no danger from the respondent. In his written version the judge mentioned C v C (Non molestation order: Jurisdiction) [1998] 1 FLR 554, FD – something he hadn't even referred to in court.

This is what singers might describe as, "A fast attitude in a slow speed." Fast like an American wise-guy in a gangster movie. Slow? Well how else could you describe the tardy delivery of the judge's ruling?

***

How would any judge feel if someone urinated outside his or her front door or if someone lit a fire in their building? Would they describe such actions as "no danger"?

Yes, for my ordeal by water was followed by ordeal by fire.

Several months after the court hearing a fire officer came to my flat while I was typing this book to explain that there was a fire in the basement of the building. This building had originally been a warehouse and was now converted into mini-loft style apartments. The fire officer told me,

"Everyone inside has to evacuate the building until the fire is out and the building secure."

Of course, I obeyed her orders, given in good faith but not accurate about the fire's location. I went downstairs to find a mixed group of residents chatter-debating outside while the small blaze was snuffed out and the building reopened. What the fire crew told us at the time and we believed was, in the words of the residents' secretary, whom you met earlier in the segment about unproven urine in the vestibule,

"The fire has been caused by mistake by workmen who are repairing - indeed reclaiming - the ground floor of the front hallway. You know what I mean. It's damaged by an unholy mix of dry rot and water-damaged timbers that's extended to the wooden joists underpinning the floor."

It was a Saturday afternoon and the workers had left for the weekend. They could not speak for themselves.

After the weekend the construction crew manager was loud in his company's defence. He had good reason for,

"The fire wasn't even in the basement like the firefighters said. And it wasn't caused by some miscellaneous spark. The fire was lit deliberately on the ground floor. Our workers had left everything intact before they left on Saturday.

"I think the fire was lit by a former resident in retaliation for being evicted."

Who knows? You see putting out the fire (which the firemen did) and repairing the damage to the ground floor (which the construction workers did) compromised the scene of the crime. To me the construction company's interpretation was more plausible than the original verdict of the fire service, which was certainly inaccurate.

I wonder how any judge would feel about a fire in his own building following a targeted urine attack? Would he suspect, would he know, who had done it?

Have family court judges even heard of, taken account of, post traumatic stress disorder among us escapees from domestic violence, we who endure the Long Domestic Abuse equivalent of Long Covid?

And if not, whatever next?

———————

Acknowledgements

I thank Keith Abbott of Michael Terence Publishing for his courage in taking on this book.

Although I wrenched subject and story of the novel from cruel experience, I needed hard lessons as how best to present the story effectively. I sought guidance from two very different Stephens, authors at opposite poles of the publishing spectrum. For insight into revving up tension I studied Stephen King, notably his *It*, (New York, 1986; large print version, RNIB, Peterborough); and for how to follow narrative and examples with hard advice, I referred to Steve Harrison, *How to Write Better Copy* (London 2016).

Among the Michael Terence Publishing team I thank designer Karolina Robinson for both her skill and craftsmanship.

Sam Helio, 2022

About the Author

Because his exciting treatment of the uncomfortable and widespread subject of domestic abuse is provocative and dangerous for him and the people around him, the author uses the pen name Sam Helio. As well as a macabre portrait of his tormentor, he targets the shortcomings of such cherished British institutions as the NHS, social services, the police and the court system.

In other books, Helio has drawn on his varied careers in the UK and the US to write histories, novels and plays. He is a committed advocate of disability rights.

*Available worldwide from
Amazon and all good bookstores*

www.mtp.agency

www.facebook.com/mtp.agency

@mtp_agency

www.ingramcontent.com/pod-product-compliance
Lightning Source LLC
LaVergne TN
LVHW041620060526
838200LV00040B/1366